Laura Richards

111
London
Pubs and Bars
That You
Shouldn't Miss

Photographs by Jamie Newson

emons:

© Photographs by Jamie Newson, except:
Headshots: Andy Parsons
© Cover motif: Shutterstock.com/danjazzia
Design: Eva Kraskes, based on a design
by Lübbeke | Naumann | Thoben
Maps: altancicek.design, www.altancicek.de
Printing and binding: CPI – Clausen & Bosse, Leck
Printed in Germany 2020
ISBN 978-3-7408-0893-8
Revised third edition, January 2020

Did you enjoy this guidebook? Would you like to see more?
Join us in uncovering new places around the world on:
www.111places.com

Foreword

While I was writing this companion to bars and pubs in one of the world's best cities for drinking, many old favourites shut up shop for good. The face of London is changing rapidly, with rising rents and small-business rates among the factors threatening to squeeze out the individuality that made writing a book like this so much fun.

But what we discovered on our travels around London was resilience, with the hard-grafting (and often eccentric) creatives behind London's best bars and pubs smiling in the face of adversity and never ducking out of their commitment to keeping the city moving, or indeed staggering. In fact, many of these publicans stepped in to save a piece of their community that may have been lost without them.

Not many things are secret in London these days, but we aimed to deliver an alternative guide to drinking, with places with a story to tell that you won't necessarily read elsewhere. Some of the London legends had to stay put; you can't write about drinking in London without the context of The Savoy's American Bar or Ye Olde Cheshire Cheese, for example. But in those instances, we've plucked out lesser-known titbits from the archives for you to discover and delve into on your boozy adventures.

In this discerning drinker's guide, you'll find wine, craft beer, ale, cocktails, gin, whisky and, err, poitín. You'll discover speakeasies, distilleries, arcades, cellars, rooftops, boats, co-ops and burlesque joints. You'll find pubs with pets, pensioners and pop stars; porn, theatre props and oddly shaped pool tables. There are toilets, post offices, garages and gambling dens turned into spruced-up watering holes. From mega-dollar haunts to spit-and-sawdust party pubs, we've embraced all styles of venue for all kinds of budget.

Now, let's drink to all 111 of these establishments staying strong against the odds for many closing times to come.

111 London Pubs and Bars

1__ The Adam & Eve

Hipsters, hops and herbs

Its L-shaped pool table is practically enough to make the trip to Homerton worth your while, but this pub has many more temptations to offer. A relief on the building's purple- and cream-tiled frontage shows Adam and Eve stood sideways on, a small sprouting tree protecting Adam's modesty. Although records date back as far as 1785 to a pub in this position, it was given the Edwardian look it still wears today in 1915 (along with that bare-all frieze). Dark wood contrasts with a pure copper ceiling that people are said to have come to admire in its own right back in the day. Original glass partitions and an island servery also remain and a raised gallery holds plenty on heaving Friday nights, with shelves for your pint wherever you roam.

The pub was given a restrained update almost 100 years on from its major 1915 renovation when new owners took over a failing business. Although Teddy Boys had visited in their droves for a boogie in the '70s, the pub had fallen out of fashion by the '90s, and the closure of nearby Hackney Hospital in 1995 contributed to the drop in footfall for the three-roomed public house. Luckily, the team who took over not only knew a thing or two about drawing a young crowd – running other pubs in London as well as Field Day music festival – but they also cared about keeping the regulars. So while DJs play music you'd find at Field Day, the pub also hosts bingo, quizzes and footie screenings, all generations happily colliding.

Although the beer garden is hardly Eden, it hosts hanging baskets and a bed where microherbs are cultivated and used on the plush menu, which Michelin-starred chef Alyn Williams helped devise when the pub relaunched. Drinking is just as delectable with a happy hour sympathetic to the area, including inexpensive Bloody Marys on Sundays – essential if you've been partying in the Adam & Eve the night before.

Address 115 Homerton High Street, E9 6AS, +44 (0)20 8985 1494, www.adamandevepub.com, info@adamandevepub.com | **Getting there** Homerton (Overground) | **Hours** Mon–Wed 4pm–11am, Thu 4pm–midnight, Fri–Sat noon–1am, Sun noon–11pm | **Tip** Combine a Sunday Bloody Mary with a trip up to Chatsworth Road Market for food, fashion and crafts. It also saw a return to glory, in 2010, after closing in the '90s.

2 Albertine

Stranger than fiction

Albertine has been around the Bush for yonks, a classic neighbour-hood bistro and wine bar that opened up in 1978. It was immedi-ately popular with workers over at the BBC Television Centre who would stop by in the headier days of business for those kinds of rosy-cheeked lunchtime meetings that ran on well into the evening. As such, it inspired the setting for what would go on to be the UK's best-known soap opera, with *EastEnders'* fictional Albert Square taking its name from this Shepherd's Bush bar. The story goes that the soap's co-creators Tony Holland and Julia Smith wrote the very first script here, and later watched the pilot episode from Alber-tine, too.

But how's this for a real-life plot twist? The bar was first opened by a lady called Sarah McEvedy but then changed hands, with Giles Philips taking charge between 1983 and 2017. But it has recently been bought by celebrity chef and food writer Allegra McEvedy – Albertine is the bar in which she grew up and in which she and her mother shared many fond memories before Sarah passed away when Allegra was just 17. Allegra – a judge on TV's *Junior Bake Off* – had stayed in touch with Philips and expressed an interest in taking the bar off his hands if it ever got to be too much. With rising London rents, he took her up on the offer.

Under the bar's new ownership, an emphasis has been put on rustic bistro dining, although Albertine remains primarily a wine bar. The walls are painted a gorgeously vinous burgundy colour, with modern artwork depicting dishes on the menu in colourful splashes. Old regulars and west Londoners hole up on the ground floor for a glass of wine and a nibble on charcuterie or drop by to buy a bottle for their evening at home, while upstairs is more dedicated to din-ing. And of course, the business meetings are still in full swing and as well lubricated as ever.

Address 1 Wood Lane, W12 7DP, +44 (0)20 8743 9593, www.albertine.london | **Getting there** Shepherd's Bush Market (Circle, Hammersmith & City Lines) | **Hours** Mon–Wed 11am–11pm, Thu–Sat 11am–midnight | **Tip** For sights more reminiscent of *EastEnders* in this corner of west London, visit Shepherd's Bush Market, open Monday to Saturday.

3__American Bar

Say cheers to the Hollywood greats

A miniature 'museum' at the foot of the American Bar and signed photographs on the corridor leading in give a hint of the glamour you're about to share with the ghosts of Hollywood. Over 125 years of history are packed into this prestigious spot, one of a handful of American-style cocktail bars that arrived on these shores at the turn of the 20th century.

Such was the popularity of the Savoy Hotel with our American cousins – its entrance the only place in the UK where you can drive on the right – that Cary Grant, Judy Garland, Fred Astaire and Elizabeth Taylor made it their home away from home. And a drink in the bar was not to be missed. Frank Sinatra kicked back with a dry martini (not the Jack Daniels you'd expect) while Marilyn Monroe drank Don Perignon with her entourage. White-jacketed bartenders became stars in their own right, such was their skill, and so the *Savoy Cocktail Book* came to be in 1930. Penned by head bartender Harry Craddock, it's a tome of the classics that had yet to be put in writing, and is still in print today.

Yet the bar never rests on its past glories. The room has hardly changed – ivory walls, patterned carpet and a baby grand piano – but the drinks list regularly shifts. Cocktails are made to reflect the day's hot topics, from a drink in honour of Princess Elizabeth's marriage, to a Moonwalk to celebrate Neil Armstrong's achievements. If you're feeling flush, you can sample the Moonwalk for £100 by ordering from the bar's vintage menu, which practically doubles as the venue's second museum to drinking. It also includes a £5000 Sazerac – when in the Savoy!

The menu, service and setting has recently earned its status as Europe's finest place to drink according to The World's 50 Best Bars. Perch on one of four stools at the bar itself to appreciate the prestige, or have your own Marilyn moment with a glass of something sparkling.

Address The Savoy Hotel, The Strand, WC2R 0EU, www.fairmont.com/savoy-london, savoy@fairmont.com | **Getting there** Covent Garden (Piccadilly Line) | **Hours** Mon–Sat 11.30am–midnight, Sun noon–midnight | **Tip** Do an 'American bar' tour – head to The Stafford hotel's version, which has been graced by Dolly Parton and Clint Eastwood.

4 Auld Shillelagh

The best Guinness in London

This may be one of London's most unassuming – perhaps even misleading – pub entrances. The tiny red-and-black frontage with just a sole picnic bench on Stoke Newington's Church Street by no means flags up what's in store for visitors. The name may hint to customers that they're in for a spot of the craic. But at first glance, you'd hardly think it were worthy of the title of the most authentic Irish pub outside of Ireland according to the *Irish Times*. But that's just what it has grown to become since the Leydon brothers – Aonghus and Tomas, from County Roscommon – took over the lease in 1991.

When the pair began at the Shillelagh, the spit-and-sawdust venue was a small room fitting that entrance, fully functioning thanks to a bar and dartboard. But in the past twenty years the pub has extended back further to accommodate its fans, creating a narrow wood-clad room now complete with a beer garden at the rear.

What makes it so authentic? For starters, a dry sense of humour from staff behind the bar, who serve pint after pint of the best-quality Guinness in London to wash down Tayto crisps. The match-day atmosphere is electric when the pub screens Irish rugby and football fixtures (or you can cheer on the pub's football team in local fixtures). You'll find regular live music nights with a traditional Gaelic band thrashing it out on the fiddle. And of course there's a whole host of characters, mostly expats who've found themselves a home away from home, The Pogues' Shane MacGowan once included.

What is most abundantly clear is that Irish party spirit, which stands firm despite the rolling tide of gentrification. Find it on Bowie or Sinatra nights or in March when the Shillelagh throws what is undoubtedly the best St Patrick's Day party in the capital. The slogan written up high above the piano in Celtic lettering says it all: *Off the leash and on the lash.*

Address 195 Stoke Newington Church Street, N16 0UD, +44 (0)20 7249 5951,
www.theauldshillelagh.co.uk, info@theauldshillelagh.co.uk | Getting there Dalston
Kingsland (Overground) | Hours Mon–Thu 11am–midnight, Fri–Sat 11am–1am,
Sun 11am–midnight | Tip Get more of a taste for Guinness at Soho's Toucan, a small
bar filled with so much signage and memorabilia, it could almost be considered a
museum for the black stuff.

5 __ Bar Américain
Classy cocktails back where they belong

It was going to take a lot for any bar to live up to this iconic location, but Bar Américain has enough swagger to pull it off. The cocktail joint is a petite room in the decadent palace that is Brasserie Zedel, a show-stopping venue that glimmers in gold, bronze and marble and harks back to Europe's grand café culture of the 1930s. Original features still stand from when the venue was a plush dining hall in the Regent Palace Hotel. The sweeping staircase sets the tone for a glitzy evening, while the bright shimmering tones of Zedel's dining hall distract from the low-lit Art Deco Bar Américain to the side, making it the perfect hideaway for a late-night rendezvous.

It's clearly a stunning destination, so why the pressure to perform? Well, this is the site of the former Atlantic Bar and Grill, home to Dick's Bar from 1994 to 2005. It's no exaggeration to say that this bar – named after its industry-leading mixologist, the late Dick Bradsell – was the place where modern bartending in London was born. Before it, nobody had such a resplendent back-bar stocked with international premium spirits and nobody was mixing them like this. The Atlantic, run by Oliver Peyton, was a destination venue and Dick's was the place where the cooler clientele holed up. Among daytime Bloody Marys and late-night martinis, people were trying cosmopolitans, Brambles and espresso martinis for the very first time (the latter two invented by Bradsell). It attracted the likes of Prince, Robert DeNiro and Michael Jordan through the door and the Spice Girls were regulars.

In 2012, the space reopened as Bar Américain and the new operators tastefully restored the bar to its former glory, laying on a menu of reasonably priced cocktail classics, from Manhattans to old-fashioneds. Guests lap up the Art Deco stylings blissfully unaware that the cocktail revolution in the capital started here.

Address 20 Sherwood Street, W1F 7ED, +44 (0)20 7734 4888, www.brasseriezedel.com, info@brasseriezedel.com | **Getting there** Piccadilly Circus (Bakerloo, Piccadilly Lines) | **Hours** Mon–Wed 4.30pm–midnight, Thu & Fri 4.30pm–1am, Sat 1pm–1am, Sun 4.30pm–11pm | **Tip** For more Art Deco decadence in the area, take a trip to Hawksmoor Air Street, part of the popular steakhouse and cocktail bar chain.

6 Bar Pepito

Costa del King's Cross

Move from the gritty streets of King's Cross to the sunny heights of southern Spain, without even boarding the Eurostar. Bar Pepito does the legwork for London-based hispanophiles, acting as an Andalucía bodega in the unlikely setting of a King's Cross courtyard. Upturned barrels have been made into tables under optimistic parasols that mark the entrance to this tiny sherry bar in a former railway storage shed. The miniature Pepito holds room for about twenty, if they don't mind compromising on personal space (as is customary on the Iberian Peninsula). To set the scene, rustic brick walls hold tall wax candles, legs of jamón hang by the bar and traditional azulito tiles in Andalucía's Moorish style brighten the room from the floor up. Authentic prints of bullfights and flamenco continue the obsession with the south of Spain, and it's all tied up with a page-turning sherry and tapas menu.

Forget the Camino de Santiago. Once you discover the 'Caminito de Pepito,' there's only one epic pilgrimage you'll want to keep making. This is the name the bar has given to its sherry-and-food-pairing menu (or 'road trip'), where adventurous sippers can indulge in six courses of tapas matched with finos, manzanillas, moscatels and more. You can simply sip on drops by the glass (with handy tasting notes on the menu), or order a flight of four sherries that are similar in style. Whatever your choice, staff encourage you to drink the tipple in the Spanish way – with a delicious snack to bring out the best in both flavours – completely dispelling the image of sherry being the preserve of grandmothers.

Bar Pepito may have kicked off one of London's more middle-class movements, a sherry revolution, when it opened its doors in 2010, but its popularity hasn't waned since the boom. Much like in Andalucía, the sun never sets on this backstreet bodega. And with King's Cross' star rising, it's a good off-the-beaten-track bar to know about.

Address 3 Varnishers Yard, The Regent Quarter, N1 9DF, +44 (0)20 7841 7331, www.camino.uk.com, kingscross@camino.uk.com | **Getting there** King's Cross St Pancras (Circle, Hammersmith & City, Metropolitan, Northern, Piccadilly, Victoria Lines, National Rail) | **Hours** Mon–Fri 5pm–midnight, Sat 6pm–midnight | **Tip** It's not the most scenic walk, but under 20 minutes away is Morito, one of London's best tapas restaurants on Exmouth Market, marvellously blending Spanish and North African flavours.

7_Bar Termini
Coffee and cocktails

A trip to Bar Termini – a bar serving sharpeners all day, from neat morning espressos to Italian aperitivi right through to negronis at dusk – is a shot in the arm. It does so in inimitable style, as an exaggerated version of the coffee bars you'd find in Rome in the 1950s, the bar's name taken from the central district of the Italian capital and its grand rail station. As such, find the knowing nod of luggage rails up above fashionable teal leather benches. A chequerboard floor, a white marble bar and staff in white coats and black ties set the monochrome mood, the overall effect as elegant as a Fellini film. How poignant that Bar Termini – which only opened in 2014 – should embrace a 1950s design, since this part of London was swimming in Italian-run bars in its post-war years when an espresso boom brought coffee-fuelled character to Soho.

It's not all retro though, thanks to third-wave coffee and futuristic booze. Marco Arrigo, founder of Islington's University of Coffee heads up the former. He's trained staff on a hybrid machine made from Faema and La Marzocco parts. The latter is the work of cocktail maestro Tony Conigliaro, who fronted a fair few London bars in the 2010s. Both have crafted anti-choice menus, with just five coffees and a smattering of cocktails.

Espresso al bar for £2.50 is designed for imbibing vertically. Caffe latte is served with steamed milk on the side for your own attempt at latte art. For something stronger, aperitivi include spritzes, martinis, Bellinis and four pre-batched versions of negronis, posters for which decorate the walls. These aren't negronis as you know them, but are cooked sous vide before batching to recreate the bottle-aging process. They're then served at the bar in delicate glassware without ice. Booking at Termini is essential, since there's only space for 25. Good things do indeed come in small packages – espressos and negronis obviously included.

Address 7 Old Compton Street, W1D 5JE, +44 (0)7841 017138, www.bar-termini-soho.com, drinks@bartermini.com | **Getting there** Tottenham Court Road (Central, Northern Lines) | **Hours** Mon–Thu 10am–11.30pm, Fri & Sat 10am–1am, Sun 11am–10.30pm | **Tip** Bar Italia wasn't quite part of the 1950s Soho espresso boom – it's been going even longer – but it's a great place to grab an authentic Italian coffee in the capital any time of day (22 Frith Street).

8 Beaufort Bar

Gilt-edged, gold-leaf Gatsby glamour

The palm-tree-lined, Art Deco entrance to the Savoy is a slice of other-era opulence rarely delivered with such sass in the capital. It's replicated – no, bettered – in the Beaufort Bar, a new addition to the hotel in 2010 that has upped the glamour ante. This dark, brooding and pure sex setting is dressed to kill in jet black and shimmering gold, a stark contrast to the delicate and airy Thames Foyer atrium from which you enter. But appropriately, this bar is only open by night, so you won't be offending any afternoon tea goers with your vampish attire should you choose to dress for the occasion (hint: you should).

Back in 2010 it was rumoured that the hotel had dropped around £38,000 on the Beaufort Bar's development. If it's true, you can tell. The gold leaf alone will have cost a bomb, glittering across the walls. Gold spirals and swirls in the black carpet, edges the tables and even catches your eye in the drinks – from blingy glasses of champagne to a cocktail actually dusted in gold leaf. The bar sits on a raised – and, you guessed it – gold platform, made from the stage that resided in this part of the hotel when it was once a cabaret club. It hosted acts like George Gershwin and Carol Gibbons, and the bar still honours the tradition with nightly live music performances.

It's the cocktails that attract the most attention, though. An award-winning bar team regularly change up the menu, and previous incarnations have included a beautiful tunnel book to illustrate drinks, or a list of cocktails inspired by magic. Or choose from a selection of story-telling drinks, each tipple weaving the narrative of an incident in the hotel's rich history or depicting the illustrious guests of yesteryear. So sip on a cocktail that recalls the time Fred Astaire danced on the roof or a drink in honour of Guccio Gucci's humble beginnings as a Savoy bellboy. This is as good as storytelling gets in a Gatsby-opulent setting.

Address The Savoy Hotel, The Strand, WC2R 0EU, +44 (0)20 7420 2111,
www.fairmont.com/savoy-london, savoy@fairmont.com | Getting there Covent Garden
(Piccadilly Line) | Hours Mon–Sat 5pm–1am | Tip For a room as dressed in gold and
as liberal with the fizz, head to Bob Bob Ricard in Mayfair. The restaurant's booths have
their own 'press for champagne' buttons.

9 Beavertown Brewery Taproom

Car park craft beer pioneers

At the start of the 2010s, a craft beer boom was about to rock London. And one of its frontmen was the son of a Led Zeppelin member. In 2011, Logan Plant (that's right, Robert Plant junior) established a microbrewery in east London's De Beauvoir Town (hence the company's Cockney name: Beavertown) inside barbecue restaurant Duke's Brew & Que. By 2014, Beavertown had moved to bigger premises in Tottenham, where it began producing cartoon-covered cans of craft beer designed by a former waiter at Duke's, Nick Dwyer.

The brewery followed a path similar to that of other craft brewers in the capital, with gradual growth leading to investment from one of the beer conglomerates – Heineken, in this case. Although some of the scene's fanatics viewed it as selling out, to many, Beavertown has managed to uphold its edgy vibe. And that's even after being made the official beer of Tottenham Hotspur when the football team opened a new stadium in 2019.

Maybe it maintains its independent streak by keeping its brewing premises and taproom in a rough-around-the-edges industrial park just up from Tottenham Hale station. There are plans in the works to launch a mega-brewery further north of London, but due to popular demand the taproom will remain. Every Saturday, the beers flow from a bar inside brewing HQ where the ceiling and walls are covered in awesome artwork by Dwyer, who is now the brand's creative director. Benches are laid out in the car park – covered by a marquee in the colder months – and are perennially packed with up to 600 devotees. They pour ten brews from keg and on the cheap, served alongside those familiar cans. There may now be over 100 breweries in the capital, but Beavertown and its punky taproom still stands out from the crowd at the end of a rocking decade for craft beer.

Address Unit 17, Lockwood Industrial Park, Mill Mead Road, London N17 9QP, +44 (0)20 8525 9884, www.beavertownbrewery.co.uk, taproom@beavertownbrewery.co.uk | Getting there Tottenham Hale (Victoria Line, National Rail) | Hours Sat noon–8pm | Tip Beavertown shares an industrial park with Pressure Drop Brewery, also open on a Saturday. Make an afternoon of it on the craft beers in Tottenham.

10___The Bedford

From courtroom to comedy club

Deluxe 4x4s glimmer in a row in the Waitrose car park opposite, a sign of the millionaires residing in this once-downtrodden neighbourhood. Yet The Bedford, a pub that dominates this busy Balham junction, couldn't be more down to earth. Locals of all ages still crowd in for unadorned drinking among the smell of pub grub – although the food is of a slightly elevated standard now. That's because, in 2019, this Grade II listed building and former hotel was restored to its past glory by Three Cheers Pub Co.

The first hint of history is rather surprising: a big-top-shaped space tucked away takes on a mock-Tudor look and calls itself the Shakespearean Globe Theatre, a joke that fits the purpose of this room as a top-drawer comedy venue. A small stage can be viewed from the floor or from tables lining a balcony around the perimeter. The bijou room is only small in size though, having hosted some of the biggest names on the comedy circuit – Stewart Lee, Catherine Tate, Harry Hill. Their framed faces make an incredible rogue's gallery on the stairwell to that balcony as well as to the music stage, the venue's other exceptional asset.

Performance is part of a tradition that's been going since the 1800s when the hotel acted as a very dramatic and well-publicised courtroom for the murder case of local cad Charles Bravo. Less dramatic but still iconic would have been a gig from U2, a band the pub boasts about having hosted back in the '70s when London's pub music scene was booming. The Clash also rocked out in Balham's Bedford, but modern stars to grace the south-west stage are more middle-of-the-road, including James Bay, Paolo Nutini and Ed Sheeran, (the latter even recording an album here). Amateurs try their luck too, with music on every week from rising stars and an open-mic stand-up comedy pit for the brave, making this the everyman pub despite its recent spruce-up.

Address 77 Bedford Hill, SW12 9HD, +44 (0)20 8682 8940, www.thebedford.com, info@thebedford.co.uk | **Getting there** Balham (Northern Line) | **Hours** Mon–Wed 3pm–midnight, Thu noon–midnight, Fri & Sat noon–2am, Sun noon–midnight | **Tip** Just up the road, the Exhibit offers another form of entertainment – a bar and restaurant that doubles as a small cinema complete with sofas.

11_ The Beer Shop

Living-room drinking

Don't let the name deceive you; this is more a bar than it is a shop. Owners Lee Gentry and Lauren Willis describe it best as a micropub. The small room just off Nunhead Green offers up four communal tables and a cluster of chairs to beer aficionados, many of whom while away an afternoon, while others stay true to the bar's name after all, stopping by for takeaway cartons of whatever's on cask.

Since the bar first opened in 2014, it's been rotating its offering every few days, but behind its small counter are just two shelves supporting four jacket-cooled casks on gravity dispense. The bar later added key keg lines to reflect London's ever-evolving beer scene, and its small room is deceptive, since hundreds of beers are listed by the bottle on a clipboard heavily loaded with pages. Breweries from far and wide are shown appreciation, but it's the local ones that prove most popular when championed by the bar or showcased at Meet the Brewer events.

Local street-food traders get support too, invited to park their vans outside. And The Beer Shop displays masterpieces by local artists on a dedicated art wall every few months, past efforts including a riff on a pie chart and a join-the-dots piece that punters are yet to crack. But the focus remains on beer above all – or 'craft not crap', as the bar states.

Locals describe The Beer Shop as epitomising 'front room drinking'. There's a regular board game night, and Takeaway Tuesdays is a reverse on the traditional BYO format, where customers can order in food like they do at home. In the summer, get involved in 'tropicale' parties or get sipping in a very beery beer garden that's been added to the rear. On Sundays you'll find neighbours with their children settling in for a session, but don't worry, there's still Led Zeppelin on the stereo. So join this married couple in treating The Beer Shop as your own sudsy living room.

Address 40 Nunhead Green, SE15 3QF, +44 (0)20 7732 5555,
www.thebeershoplondon.co.uk, hello@thebeershop.co.uk | **Getting there** Nunhead
(National Rail) | **Hours** Tue–Thu 4–11pm, Fri 4–11.30pm, Sat noon–11.30pm, Sun
noon–8pm | **Tip** Hop, Burns and Black is a bottle shop down the road towards East
Dulwich so you can do even more living-room drinking.

12 Black Friar

Next level Art Nouveau

A pub owned by the Nicholson's group on a smoggy junction facing Blackfriars station doesn't sound like much to go on, but this is one of London's most iconic buildings offering an unparalleled drinking experience. The Black Friar is a little slice of London heritage, a wedge-shaped pinnacle of international Art Nouveau, the likes of which still get the knickers of London architects in a twist. All the intricacies (dating from 1905, when the building was remodelled) pay homage to the site's previous purpose as a Dominican monastery, and the first sign you'll see of this is the friar himself in statue form, jovially hanging from the corner of the pub, mouth upturned. That cheeky grin is probably because he knows what beauty lies within.

It's possible that newcomers won't chance upon the secrets of the pub's inner sanctum, since they are to be found in the rear room behind a bar that splits the pub in half. Persevere to discover the maddest decorative reliefs, mosaic ceilings and copper friezes by sculptural artist Henry Poole, depicting the life of monks in ornate and astonishing detail, along with mottos in large font: 'Silence is golden' standing out in particular.

Much of Poole's work has been lost over time with the destruction of the buildings that contained them, and for a period it seemed the Black Friar's fate would be the same with plans for demolition and redevelopment in the '60s. A fervent campaign was mounted to save the pub – notably spearheaded by Poet Laureate Sir John Betjeman – and it now has Grade II-listed status protecting it and a happy mix of drinkers who frequent it.

Find City workers swaying around, tourists drinking tea and commuters enjoying a pre-train pint. In summer, they'll often join that jolly friar outside on a rather unpleasant, traffic-facing terrace. But that only leaves the beautiful interior to the savvy drinkers.

Address 174 Queen Victoria Street, EC4V 4EG, +44 (0)20 7236 5474, www.nicholsonspubs.co.uk | **Getting there** Blackfriars (National Rail, Circle, District Lines) | **Hours** Mon–Sat 9am–11pm, Sun noon–10.30pm | **Tip** Venture to nearby St Paul's Cathedral to enjoy more of Poole's unique sculptural work.

13 Black Rock
Got wood?

If Black Rock were a person, you'd want to date it. The bar, founded in 2016, is sharp and sophisticated, dressed to kill in black; it's quietly confident about one of the finest whisky collections in town; and it has something truly unique to offer – an 18-foot hunk from a 185-year-old English oak tree running through the room.

But what's the wood all about? Two channels have been carved within this grand old oak, filled with the spirit and covered with glass. So on the one hand, this big block acts as a fairly unconventional table. But on the other hand, these channels act as 'Whisky Rivers' – one lined with French limousin oak carrying an ever-evolving 'table whisky', and the other a flavoured version with cherry and mint among past ingredients. Taps are fixed to this ornate log for access to London's two finest rivers (sorry, River Thames, you came a close third).

Black Rock doesn't stop there in its quest to deliver a good dram. Three glass cabinets present around 250 bottles from global distilleries. Rather than group them by country, whiskies are organised by flavour profile – spice, fruit, smoke etc. Find a whisky you love, and chances are you'll like its neighbouring bottle. They're all labelled with black dots to indicate the price – £7, £9 or £11 a snifter. And individual copper taps are fitted to tables for those after a spot of dilution with their sipping.

Finally, a trolley is used for mixing top-drawer cocktails, including a list of five highballs (whisky, mixer and bitters). Indeed, there's actually no bar, with two members of staff parading the room and offering advice. They've learned from experts Tristan Stephenson and Tom Aske, who have let their whisky concept develop and mature. It now includes a further tavern above and 'whisky lodgings' on the next floor up. When these boutique rooms launch in 2020, Black Rock will be London's first whisky hotel. There's no doubt that Black Rock is singlehandedly shaking off the spirit's fusty reputation.

Address 9 Christopher Street, EC2A 2BS, +44 (0)20 7247 4580, www.blackrock.bar, hello@blackrock.bar | Getting there Liverpool Street (Central, Circle, Hammersmith & City, Metropolitan Lines, Overground) | **Hours** Mon–Wed 5pm–midnight, Thu 5pm–1am, Fri & Sat 5pm–2am | **Tip** For more whisky sipping in the neighbourhood, try Bull in a China Shop on Shoreditch High Street, shining a light on Japanese drams.

14_Bricklayer's Arms

Real ale, real good times

'London's permanent beer festival', says The Brick's website. In a city that's been through a beer revolution, that's a bold statement. But this old-style Putney pub isn't talking about hipster-enticing events. The sort of beer festival it brings to mind is in a yeasty tent in a field. The Bricklayer's Arms is celebrating traditional British ale-making, shining a light on the likes of Timothy Taylor, Windsor & Eton, Downton and Twickenham breweries. But they'll often have something from London's By the Horns Brewing Co. for those committed to craft beer.

This rather old-fashioned approach to drinking is mirrored in the pub's appearance. It sits as a red and cream anomaly surrounded by drab-looking buildings. You get the feeling the place hasn't changed much since its days as a coaching inn and blacksmith's forge. It's been a public house since 1826 when it was known as the Waterman's Arms. The pub changed its name later that century to fit the construction workers building the District Line who would come by to talk shop. Then, in 2002, young couple John and Helen Newman bought the place when it went up for auction, saving it from redevelopment. After six months in operation, they decided to turn the pub into their family home, but after Helen passed away in 2005 John needed to find a way to provide for his two young boys. Helen's sister, Becky Newman, stepped in to help bring the pub back to life, opening to a large crowd on Boat Race day.

Find wood-clad walls, bar skittles and newspaper clippings that tell of yesteryear as lovingly as reviews on The Brick's website, a seemingly buzzing forum and testament to the pub's community. They claim personalities ranging from blues musicians to Great Train Robbers to actor-gangster John Bindon used to frequent the pub. But they also tell of friendships past, and more recent sessions where they've practically drunk the bar dry.

Address 32 Waterman Street, SW15 1DD, +44 (0)20 8785 4344, www.bricklayers-arms.co.uk |
Getting there Putney (National Rail) | **Hours** Mon–Thu 4–11pm, Fri & Sat noon–11pm,
Sun noon–10.30pm | **Tip** The Great British Beer Festival runs every August at Olympia and
has been serving up the best suds for over 40 years.

15__Café Kick

Football crazy, foosball mad

With its Formica tables, scuffed yellow walls and wooden floor-boards, Café Kick comes off a bit like one of those slightly naff continental bar-cafés you'd find in rural Spain or Italy. But it's filled with a young crowd of low-key London lads as well as travellers who've heard of its worth through the grapevine. The outcome is somewhere between Benidorm and Berlin. Brexit is definitely a bad word at Café Kick.

You'd be blind not to notice the footballing theme. Everywhere you turn there's a symbol of worship. The walls are emblazoned with niche teams' scarves (from Hellas Verona F.C. to FC St. Pauli) and the ceiling is decorated in international flags, which have all been added since the bar launched back in 1997 (just beyond the glory days of Euro 96). Fans of the bar as well as the beautiful game have donated these emblems to Café Kick, along with their foreign currency added to a collage of notes pinned up behind the bar. You can catch action from La Liga and the like from any corner of the room, yet if you're not here to bow down to Balotelli and the boys, television sets remain relatively discreet with the sound muted in favour of music.

The space used to be a toyshop on London's beautiful Exmouth Market stretch. It's a cute history, given that Café Kick's ultimate obsession is grown-up gaming. The bar's owners brought to London their love for French 'baby foot' (or table football, in other words), placing three vintage Bonzini tables made in France in the room. The bar's popularity meant that a second, larger foosball bar – Bar Kick – arrived in Shoreditch in 2001. But if you're after something more fanatical and further off the beaten track, the original wins this penalty shootout. Visit during one of the capital's most generous happy hours – where bottles of beer are served at Europe-friendly prices – to soak up the match-day action at its truest.

Address 43 Exmouth Market, EC1R 4QL, +44 (0)20 7837 8077, www.cafekick.co.uk |
Getting there Angel (Northern Line) | **Hours** Mon–Thu 11am–11pm, Fri & Sat
11am–midnight, Sun noon–10.30pm | **Tip** If table football isn't your thing, stick to
table tennis at Old China Hand, a down-to-earth and entertaining pub round the
corner (8 Tysoe Street).

16___CellarDoor

Lewd drinks in a former public loo

Five or ten years ago, opening a bar in a former public lavatory was a fairly revolutionary act. But while London may be fit to bursting with WC watering holes these days, few have the flair of CellarDoor, a reliable old loo underneath The Strand that first opened for a very different kind of business in 2006.

Venture down the stairs and knock on the door, where a Prohibition-style eye slit will be drawn back for scrutiny, but staff are pretty welcoming once you enter the tiny basement bar. Much has been done to make the intimate space seem expansive, with mirrored walls casting a dazzling illusion. Banquettes are styled into mouth and bum shapes to set that playful tone, and the menu of drinks continues in a similar ape. Champagne cocktails take their name from right-on feminists while a Spice Boys cocktail (complete with Thai chilli tincture) will get the party started.

The story goes that Oscar Wilde frequented the venue in its former life (for what purpose, we couldn't possibly comment). You probably won't find any major thinkers or literary legends propping up the bar today, but you can expect mind-altering antics in abundance. This is in small part due to those cheeky drinks, but Cellar-Door also lays on a flirty roster of burlesque and drag acts in a setting that's so intimate, you're sure to get a lot of bang for your buck. They even offer cinema screenings on a Sunday and put their own slant on afternoon tea on Saturdays, with a blend of burlesque, blackjack and finger sandwiches.

Befitting the venue, the toilets happen to be quite the talking point. Here you'll get more of a show than you'll find in the rest of the West End, since toilet doors are transparent. Don't worry if that gives you bathroom stage fright – the lock of the door magically turns the glass opaque, affording a bit of privacy to those punters prepared to spend a penny.

Address 0 Aldwych, WC2E 7DN, +44 (0)20 7240 8848, www.cellardoor.biz, angel@cellardoor.biz | **Getting there** Covent Garden (Piccadilly Line) | **Hours** Mon–Fri 4pm–1am, Sat 6pm–1am, Sun 6pm–midnight | **Tip** If you're after toilet-dwelling in daylight hours, The Attendant is just a twenty-minute walk away in Fitzrovia. Enjoy a subterranean cup of Joe by the old urinals of this modern café.

17__Chesham Arms

Cherished backstreet boozer saved by locals

It's hard to feel a sense of community in such a sprawling city, but regulars at the Chesham Arms know a thing or two about it. The most loyal of the lot clubbed together in 2012 to save their local after a new landlord boarded up the building on this Victorian terrace in Hackney. He had plans to turn it into offices and luxury flats, tearing out the original bar of this 150-year-old pub in the process. Campaigners fought a legal battle for two long years under the 'Save the Chesham' banner and in 2014 the council finally made the pub an asset of community value, preventing it from becoming anything other than a pub. The final victory came in 2015 when the landlord agreed a 15-year lease with local publican Andy Bird, who lovingly restored the Chesham to its present glory.

All the hallmarks of an age-old London pub are present but with a cool-enough edge to attract the area's thirty-something drinkers (and their very trendy dogs). This starts with the pretty grey-purple paint job and gold lettering on the outside and leads to tasteful red walls and aged oak floorboards inside. TV sets have been scrapped in favour of chat, and the atmosphere is made all the warmer by two log fires. There's even a verdant walled garden with picnic benches and parasols.

That restored bar hosts a challenging list of craft beers and ales, which lures in local CAMRA members and beer bloggers on quieter nights. And hip wine magazine *Noble Rot* put together the wine list when the pub first opened. Pizzas can be ordered in from nearby champs Yard Sale, completing the tasty line-up at this perfect pub with a modern-day edge.

The Chesham Arms has gone from strength to strength since reopening, the cherry on the cake being a regional Pub of the Year accolade from CAMRA in 2016. They clearly fell in love with the country feel of what must be London's best backstreet pub.

Address 15 Mehetabel Road, E9 6DU, +44 (0)20 8986 6717, www.cheshamarms.com, joe@cheshamarms.com | **Getting there** Hackney Central (Overground) | **Hours** Mon–Thu 4.30–11pm, Fri–Sun noon–11pm | **Tip** If pizza won't cut it, head to Peg on Morning Lane, a thoroughly modern restaurant elevating food on a stick to a whole new level.

18__Churchill Arms

Chelsea Flower Show's got nothing on this

With all the ancient pubs in the City and by the docks, the likes of which you'd read of in *A Christmas Carol*, you'd never guess that a Kensington tavern could have earned the accolade of 'London's most festive pub'. But the tabloids went mad for the Churchill Arms' winter display in 2016 when Irish landlord Gerry O'Brien covered the pub with a total of 90 Christmas trees and 21,000 lights, making it more resplendent by night than nearby Harrods. It's usually the pub's springtime appearance that gathers column inches and attracts the camera-wielding tourists. The Churchill allocates a reported £25,000 a year to decorating its exterior in blossoming flowers bursting from window boxes and hanging baskets, and draped from the many tiers of the handsome building. That means that the pub has managed to win prizes at Chelsea Flower Show time and time again without even having a garden.

The Churchill also claims to be London's first pub to serve Thai food – a cuisine type now ubiquitous in pubs – in its rear restaurant also wildly decorated in vines, palms and flower arrangements. But that doesn't mean that traditions are forgotten, with ales on draught and chunks of cheese and crisps in bowls on the bar. After all, this is a pub renamed out of pure patriotism following World War II. Every year, it celebrates the late Prime Minister's birthday in November with a big bash and live music, but it's not based on pure whimsy – Winston Churchill's grandparents actually used to be regulars here.

What is whimsical though is the interior design. It's a collector's wet dream, with pots, pans, clocks, medals, Airfix models, wartime memorabilia and Churchill emblems fixed to the walls or swinging from the rafters. Gerry, who has just retired after 32 years at the helm, certainly made the place look unique. And if the decorations don't warm you, mischievous chatter from sprightly old-timers will.

Address 119 Kensington Church Street, W8 7LN, +44 (0)20 7727 4242, www.churchillarmskensington.com, churchillarms@fullers.co.uk | **Getting there** Notting Hill Gate (Central, Circle, District Lines) | **Hours** Mon – Wed 11am – 11pm, Thu – Sat 11am – midnight, Sun noon – 10.30pm | **Tip** Just off Kensington Church Street is Maggie Jones's restaurant, another kooky venue, which takes its name from Princess Margaret and has a ceiling similarly covered in curious knickknacks.

19__The City Barge

Beatles and boats

This posh west London pub might be in its infancy in its current guise, but The City Barge has been going for a lot longer than it first lets on. If you need proof, just check The Beatles' 1965 movie *Help!*, in which the boys from the band scamper into one of London's finest riverside pubs so Ringo Starr can order 'Two lagers and lime and two lagers and lime'. It's just that Metropolitan Pub Company took on the business in 2014, reopening the Barge with a tasteful look that paid homage to the building's origins as a 14th-century public house as well as to how it was in its Victorian prime, when it changed its name to mirror the Lord Mayor's boat that was moored in the area. Don't expect to find a Beethoven-loving tiger in the basement as in *Help!* If a basement existed, it would surely get flooded, with this section of Chiswick's Strand-On-The-Green a victim of spring's high tide.

The City Barge's riverside location is what makes it so pleasant though, with views out to Oliver's Island (a tiny, bushy eyot where Oliver Cromwell was rumoured to have hidden during the English Civil War) and Kew Rail Bridge. If punters enter from the riverside, the daily weather forecast and high tide are advertised on a blackboard. Parquet floorboards and a grand chandelier add character indoors, with gingham furniture fitting the postcode. The lower ground is reserved for dining on steaks and fishcakes with catches of the day sourced from Billingsgate market, while upstairs is fit for banquets, with a balcony overlooking rowers practicing laps for the Boat Race. The pub doesn't rely on its rock 'n' roll history; you won't find Ringo, Paul, John and George framed on the walls. Instead, it celebrates the area's watery life with a metre-long Thames barge behind glass and with black-and-white pictures of old Chiswick decorating the walls. Or paintings of otters. And otters trump Beatles, every time.

Address 27 Strand-on-the-Green, W4 3PH, +44 (0)20 8994 2148, www.citybargechiswick.com, info@citybargechiswick.com | **Getting there** Gunnersbury (District Line, Overground) | **Hours** Mon–Thu noon–11pm, Fri noon–midnight, Sat 10am–midnight, Sun 10am–10.30pm | **Tip** Chiswick House is where the Beatles filmed the videos for 'Paperback Writer' and 'Rain' in 1966. Go visit the gardens.

20 City of London Distillery Bar

Gin served straight from the source

London's craft gin craze is in full swing, but look back five years and only a handful of producers were making the spirit in small batches within the M25. One of the frontrunners was City of London Distillery, who not only hold the title of being the first to make gin in the Square Mile in over 200 years, but also claim to be the only producer of anything within the City, a feat that has officially earned them the right to carry the prestigious area's crest on bottles. The space owned by Jonathan Clarke was once the snooker club where he was employed in 1976 as a 16-year-old. He earned £32.50 a week washing pots, a wage he paid homage to as master distiller by pricing City of London Dry Gin at £32.50 a bottle when it was first released in 2012.

Lucky for Londoners, there's a gin bar attached to the Bride Lane distillery. Known as COLD Bar for short, the smart room suits the area well, with tall-backed armchairs and mahogany and jade hues giving the room library levels of authority. The absence of cigar smoke feels at odds with the gentlemen's club aesthetic. Bar staff are dressed in herringbone waistcoats and sure enough, many punters are as suited and booted as the tweed-clad staff, choosing COLD as their after-work club. But you'll also find couples on dates and groups of friends making the day trip to London to see this ginstitution at work.

While you drink cocktails based on one of the brand's eight batches, you can gaze at the copper stills that make the magic happen. The two stills were custom-made in Germany and shipped over to the bar, and are displayed behind glass at the rear of the room. They've been given the lovable names of Clarissa and Jennifer after TV's *Two Fat Ladies*. Get better acquainted with the pair on one of the distillery's tastings, or just get sozzled in the midst of city slickers instead.

Address 22–24 Bride Lane, EC4Y 8DT, +44 (0)20 7936 3636,
www.cityoflondondistillery.co.uk, bookings@cityoflondondistillery.com | Getting there
Blackfriars (Circle, District Lines, National Rail) | Hours Mon–Sat 4–11pm | Tip
Get to grips with mother's ruin by booking on Gin Journey, an afternoon of educational
drinking in either Shoreditch, Bermondsey or Soho (www.ginjourney.com/uk/london).

21 The Clifton

From 'hotel' to charming hostelry

When you think of St John's Wood, you probably think of Lord's Cricket Ground or of tourists striding across Abbey Road like it's going out of fashion (guys, it is). Otherwise, this leafy part of town is best associated with an average house price of £1.5m. That's what makes the tale of The Clifton so surprising. A historic pub and hotel (with absolutely no guest rooms) has just come out of a three-year battle against its development into a mega mansion.

The Clifton first stood as a lodge in 1846 on what had been Henry VIII's hunting grounds, obtaining an ale licence in 1889. So what's all this 'hotel' business about? The story goes that Edward VII and his mistress Lillie Langtry chose The Clifton as a place to conduct some of their many rendezvous. It was outlawed for royalty to be seen in public houses, and so the king is said to have changed its name to The Clifton Hotel. Even in an area that has counted Sir Richard Branson, Kate Moss and Sir Paul McCartney as residents, that's quite a bit of local history and enough to convince Westminster Council to block developments by issuing an asset of community value order.

After significant work to a building that had stood empty for over three years, The Clifton is back in action and in no doubt about its status as a pub, not a hotel. Local brothers Ben and Ed Robson have taken on a 20-year lease, after closing their schnitzel and spritz joint Boopshis in Fitzrovia to focus on the pub. They've taken on a chef from famed Providores restaurant to provide poshed-up pub grub to suit the neighbourhood, and they've kitted out the interior in smart green and grey, keeping original features including a grand old fireplace. A beer garden sits out front facing a street lined with unbelievable cars. A picture of Bertie hangs on the wall in honour of that history, which staff are more than happy to fill you in on.

Address 96 Clifton Hill, NW8 0JT, +44 (0)20 7625 5010, www.thecliftonnw8.com, info@thecliftonnw8.com | Getting there St John's Wood (Jubilee Line) | Hours Mon–Sat 10am–11pm, Sun noon–10.30pm | Tip For more culture in the area, visit the Ben Uri Museum, which looks at migration and identity through visual arts (or go to that Abbey Road zebra crossing, we won't judge!).

22 Compton Arms

Orwell's old favourite

Even though George Orwell knew a thing or two about good London boozers, the writer's perfect pub, 'The Moon Under Water', didn't make the cut for this book. But that's because it never existed. The pub whose atmosphere he praised so heavily in an essay published in the *Evening Standard* in 1946 had a Victorian interior, a roaring fire in winter, courteous staff, great bar snacks and stout on draught. This pub of dreams might have been fictitious, but many have since speculated that the Compton Arms, one of Orwell's regular haunts, was pretty close to this ideal. And the pint-sized Islington inn has had a recent update that brings out the best of its original qualities while adding some sensitive modern touches.

It's now run by Nick Stephens, a landlord who owns an even smaller pub in Hackney. In 2014 he took on the lease of The Gun and made it into a 'proper pub' with a focus on beer and bar snacks. And so, in 2018, that also became the philosophy at the Compton – a former Greene King boozer and match-day hangout that had become a bit unloved before closing down. Under Stephens' wing, though, this free house now offers a range of ales and London craft beers on draught, delicious cocktails made from a far-from-bog-standard mix of spirits, and spectacular meaty grub coming out of the kitchen courtesy of resident restaurant Four Legs (which takes its name from Orwell's famous *Animal Farm* adage: 'four legs good, two legs bad').

But really, it's the atmosphere – just what Orwell was obsessed with – that makes this place so special. It's still a Gunners haven (although a little less rowdy these days). There's a walled beer garden out the back, and in winter, the small rooms get awfully cosy, with bullseye glass windows steaming up a treat. Who needs The Moon Under Water when there's this slice of contemporary pub perfection in London?

Address 4 Compton Avenue, N1 2XD, +44 (0)20 7354 8473, www.comptonarms.co.uk, comptonarms@localsclub.co.uk | **Getting there** Highbury & Islington (Victoria, Overground Lines) | **Hours** Mon–Thu 3–11pm, Fri 3pm–12.30am, Sat noon–12.30, Sun noon–11.30pm | **Tip** Orwell was also said to soak up the atmosphere at nearby pub The Canonbury, where he supposedly penned some of '1984' in the beer garden.

23 Connaught Bar
Superstar martinis

Sipping on martinis in a high-end hotel may sound like an old-fashioned cliché straight from an Ian Fleming novel, but there's nothing unoriginal about drinking in the Connaught Bar. The 5-star Connaught hotel in Mayfair has won gong after gong for the second of its bars since it reopened in 2008. You can't help but think that its popularity stems from its nifty martini trolley. Wheeled over to your table to help you customise your cocktail, it really is the ultimate luxury in drinking.

But it's mostly down to Agostino Perrone, the bar's director of mixology who hails from Lake Como, a part of the world not exactly renowned for its cocktail flair. But Ago came to London in 2003 and soon ascended to the top of the capital's cocktail-making scene. He was building on that reputation at Montgomery Place in Notting Hill (a bar once famed but now closed) when he got the call to help relaunch the Connaught Bar. He's been here ever since and with it has helped challenge the perception of hotel bars altogether, earning himself the title of International Bartender of the Year along the way. His exacting standards will make you wonder why you bother getting out of bed in the morning, and with his slick Italian team there's never a drop put wrong as they pour megadollar cocktails for megadollar customers.

At the Connaught Bar they've turned the Bloody Mary on its head serving it with 'celery air,' and as they pour your martini from a height and offer to up the ante on your favourite botanical you question how you'll ever drink one anywhere else again. They even have a custom-ised stamp to brand whopping great ice cubes with The Connaught's logo. The room shimmers with silver highlights and light bounces from large mirrors, cementing the sophistication. So if you get one pricey cocktail in the capital, it's well worth making it a martini at The Connaught. Go on, get trollied.

Address The Connaught, Carlos Place, W1K 2AL, +44 (0)20 7314 3419,
www.the-connaught.co.uk | Getting there Bond Street (Central, Jubilee Lines) | Hours
Mon – Sat 4pm – 1am, Sun 4pm – midnight | Tip The hotel also offers Michelin-star dining
at Helene Darroze at The Connaught. The weekday lunch menu is just about affordable.

24_ The Craft Beer Co. Clerkenwell

One for the beer nerds

Some may sneer at London mark-ups when they spot pints around the £8 mark at Craft Beer Co.'s flagship pub. But fans of the brand know they're paying a premium for quality. Craft Beer Co. is showcasing unique finds from around the world for the hopheads of London, the first place in the capital to go all-out geeky with its artisanal selection. We're talking 16 on cask, 21 on keg and over 200 by the bottle, the most extensive range of craft beer in the UK when it first opened in 2011 (only to be outdone by a second branch in Covent Garden in 2014). It's hardly overstating things to suggest that this pub was in part responsible for the proliferation of the term 'craft beer'.

Founder Martin Hayes had been warming up over at Pimlico's Cask Pub & Kitchen, which opened in 2009 and gave him the blueprint for the company: sourcing beers the likes of which you just wouldn't ordinarily find in the UK by cutting out wholesalers on imports. The CBC strategy proved popular, with eight other pubs now in the group.

Yet there were two objectives to the mission – a thoroughly modern drinks list needed to be teamed with old-school pub values. Spy it from the exterior, which gives the illusion of any traditional City pub thanks to racing-green tiles and flowering plant pots. Inside, a muted colour scheme is offset by bold stained glass, a red-tiled fireplace and ruby stools. Look up – perhaps in thanks to the beer gods – and you'll see a stunning mirrored and wood-carved ceiling from this pub's days as the Clock House inn, a grand chandelier its centerpiece and numerals round it like those on a clock face. Pass the time merrily digesting the daily beer list, including one-keg wonders from Down Under, and beers from established and fledgling world breweries.

Address 82 Leather Lane, EC1N 7TR, +44 (0)20 7404 7049, www.thecraftbeerco.com, clerkenwell@thecraftbeerco.com | **Getting there** Farringdon (Circle, Hammersmith & City, Metropolitan Lines, National Rail) | **Hours** Mon–Sat noon–11pm, Sun noon–10.30pm | **Tip** Coffee gets put on a pedestal in the same way as craft beer at Leather Lane neighbour Prufrock Coffee. Sample beans from all over Europe served at their best in London.

25__Crate Brewery

Canalside brewery, bar and barge

In the shadow of the successes of London's Olympic Games in 2012, Crate Brewery opened and became yet another triumph for the once-neglected Hackney Wick 'hood. Cropping up in tall art studio the White Building, this brewery, taproom and pizzeria is perfectly placed on the bank of the Lea Navigation and looks a picture as drinkers occupy picnic benches by the canal or in the juxtaposed car park with its stark graffiti and surrounding warehouses.

Just as picturesque is Crate's interior, with furniture and fixtures made from debris found around Hackney Wick. The founders, siblings and Kiwis Jess and Tom Seaton, teamed up with local artists to transform railway sleepers and ladders into seats, sandbags into sofas and bedsprings into light fittings. The overall effect is rugged chic with sustainability at its core. They also teamed up with Neil Hinchley to make first-rate beer at a time when the craft beer revolution showed no signs of slowing. Crate is now in good supply at some of the best bars around town, but trying their Golden Ale as fresh as it comes is a proper treat. The brand's success has seen the microbrewery (once viewable from within the taproom) move from the White Building to a neighbouring warehouse they've renamed the Brew Shed.

Success comes in other forms, with a sister venue across the car park. Mick's Garage opened in 2015 and showcases London's first kombucha bar (a pokey-tasting fermented tea that's now all the rage in London). And 2016 saw the launch of a boat bar too, with a handsome blue barge, the Alfred Leroy, doing cocktail cruises or parking up by the White Building. And things just keep on getting better: in 2019, the UK's first zero-waste restaurant Silo moved in to the shared space and got London's food critics into a frenzy. Exciting stuff is happening here, for sure, and a pint by the canal at Crate couldn't be any more energising.

Address 7 The White Building, Queen's Yard, E9 5EN, +44 (0)20 8533 3331, www.cratebrewery.com, info@cratebrewery.com | **Getting there** Hackney Wick (Overground) | **Hours** Mon–Thu noon–11pm, Fri & Sat noon–midnight, Sun noon–11pm | **Tip** Have a Hackney Wick brewery crawl – Howling Hops Brewery and Tank Bar is in the same industrial park and serves zesty, hop-forward pints aplenty.

26__Crobar

Heavy metal melting pot on the outskirts of Soho

Crobar's exterior tells it all. Its pavements are almost permanently decorated with interesting and hairy characters dressed in denim and covered in tats, a drawing of a skull emblazons the entrance and large, rebellious lettering spells out: *Beer 'n' whiskey. Rock 'n' roll.* The modus operandi has been clear since day one when Rich and Steve, friends and former employees at nearby music venue The Borderline, set up shop in Soho in 2001. The pair had struggled to find anywhere offering a middle ground between a bar and a nightclub. So they set out to establish a place where the jukebox was packed with classic rock and far-from-mainstream metal and the bar was stocked heavily with bourbon (the house drink) and beer. The late-night operating hours helped seal Crobar's reputation as a rocking venue for left-field thrill-seekers. Before the Astoria shut down, this was *the* pre- and post-gig hangout for serious shenanigans until 3am.

It seems apt that the bar goes against the grain on Manette Street. This part of town is where the London Anarchist Group held meetings in the '50s, while the building itself used to belong to flamboyant drag star Danny La Rue. There's no dress code at Crobar, but rather an attitude code. Rich says anyone is welcome, just as long as they 'aren't up their own arse' and are up for a good time. A drop-in from mainstream rebel Justin Bieber provoked mixed reactions from regulars. More welcome past guests include Jack Black and members of Iron Maiden and Metallica, with Dave Grohl coming in for a chat at the bar about things as British as the weather (despite being thrown out on his first visit for setting off the fire alarm three times in 20 minutes). Most of the fun had here has been minus the celebs, though, in this ever-colourful watering hole where punters are reassured that what happens at Crobar stays at Crobar.

Address 17 Manette Street, W1D 4AS, +44 (0)20 7439 0831, www.crobar.co.uk, thecrobarsoho@hotmail.com | **Getting there** Tottenham Court Road (Central, Northern Lines) | **Hours** Mon–Sat 4pm–3am | **Tip** A similarly edgy crowd is often found at nearby Garlic & Shots. The Frith Street joint with a name that says it all has been going for about as long as Crobar.

27 — Dalston Eastern Curve Garden

Dig the community vibe

It can feel surprisingly warm and fuzzy drinking in the great outdoors in east London. Dalston Eastern Curve Garden cropped up in the summer of 2010, a community space with a garden café serving wine, locally brewed beer and mulled cider in the winter, with all money from the bar being put back into the green space.

Directly opposite Dalston Junction Station, Hackney Peace Carnival Mural – a local artwork celebrating harmony between the area's mixed communities – marks the entrance to the gorgeous garden. It's a symbolic entryway, as Curve Garden is all about the community vibes. It's tended to by a group of local volunteers who assemble every Saturday to busy their green fingers with gardening projects. The space hosts charitable events and once a week, a group with learning difficulties gathers in the garden to play music.

Architectural collective Exzyt designed the look for the disused space, part of the Eastern Curve railway line that closed in 1944, and compared with the gritty streets, this is a miniature Eden. Vegetables from artichoke to celeriac line up in beds with flowers, and a canopy of trees shelters picnic benches, with bunting strewn through branches. Two giant figures by graffiti artist Stik meld urban with pastoral.

The Garden Café is housed under a wooden pavilion where food and drink are served in the week, Latto's Pizzas producing sourdough creations from a wood-fired oven every weekend. In the winter, they give out hot-water bottles, blankets and even Stanley the cat for warmth, while annual pumpkin lantern displays and a Festival of Light brighten up the colder months. And drinking in this blissful space in the summer easily beats a bottle of warm beer in London's other ever-mobbed parks.

Address 13 Dalston Lane, E8 3DF, www.dalstongarden.org | Getting there Dalston
Junction (Overground) | Hours Mon–Wed 11am–7pm, Thu–Sun 11am–11pm | Tip
There are even more outdoor antics at Dalston Roof Park round the corner, a place to get
high with DJs and drinks.

28__The Distillery

Four floors of mother's ruin

The Distillery is more than a gin bar; it's practically a way of life. This four-storey townhouse on Portobello Road is the world's first 'gin hotel', with a bar, restaurant, museum and boutique bedrooms spread across the juniper-loving premises.

Although the gin hotel only opened its doors to the public – and to much fanfare – at the end of 2016, The Distillery started out as a different concept down the road in 2011. It was at no. 171 that Portobello Road Gin was born inside the brand's very own gin museum, The Ginstitute, which was in turn housed above the group's bar, the Portobello Star (are you keeping up?). As Portobello Road Gin gained in popularity and as the gin craze swept across London, a larger site dedicated to mother's ruin became a no-brainer. Now ginthusiasts can book in for an overnight session on the drink du jour as well as a spot of gin-making in the Ginstitute, which has moved to join the boozy flagship.

GinTonica on the first floor is the most enjoyable space if it's just a drink you're after. It takes influence from Spain's love of a good G&T, with drinks served in large *copa de balón* glasses so you can have an authentically strong sip from a goblet-sized vessel. They come stuffed with so many garnishes that staff describe them as 'gin salads'. Be sure to order tapas on the side in this bright room with the colour scheme of Gaudi's Park Güell. A more trad drinking experience is found in the ground floor's Resting Room, which puts less emphasis on gin, with barrels of assorted booze ageing above the bar and used in inventive cocktails.

Pedants will note that the brand's gin is no longer made on the road where it was conceived, since the operation has expanded. But that doesn't make the experience any less iconic. Overnight stays in their boutique rooms with enviable mini bars will set you back, but you'll need a lie down after all that mother's ruin.

Address 186 Portobello Road, W11 1LA, +44 (0)20 3034 2233, www.the-distillery.london, info@the-distillery.london | Getting there Ladbroke Grove (Circle, Hammersmith & City Lines) | Hours The Resting Room, Mon–Sat 11am–midnight, Sun 11am–11pm; GinTonica, Mon & Tue 4pm–1am, Wed–Sat noon–1am, Sun noon–midnight | Tip For more gin-distilling history, take a tour of Sipsmith's plummy headquarters in Chiswick.

29__ The Dolphin

Who knew the dolphin was such a party animal?

When everywhere else is drawing down the blinds, Hackney's night owls make a beeline for The Dolphin. It's a pub famous for the kind of things other places probably wouldn't boast about – late opening hours, terrible tunes, a boisterous crowd, karaoke and *serious* drinking – yet somehow this rough-around-the-edges pub wears it so well. In fact, it wears it like a badge of honour on its unofficial but officially hilarious Twitter account where its bio invites you to 'Imagine the best fucking pub ever. Then times it by a billion'. While all its neighbours are trying to be cool, this old-school pub laughs rebelliously in the face of trends.

A pub has stood here since 1850, and although the red-and-black façade looks tired, elements of The Dolphin's historic interior have been lovingly protected and have gained the pub its Grade II listing. Find old oak partitions and parquet floorboards, plus astonishing tiling on the walls depicting scenes from Greek mythology. Just as legendary is the sight of bodies grinding to RnB and cheesy pop until 4am on Saturdays in among the seedy red ceiling, matching carpets and marble columns.

Such a sight could have been as mythical as those murals, as the police requested a review of the pub's licence and restricted its opening hours back in 2013 after a spate of reported thefts. Husband-and-wife team Yasir 'Yash' and Nuvit Yildiz (who tied the knot in the pub, such is their love for the place) launched a 'Save the Dolphin' campaign and successfully appealed against the restricted opening hours. An experience here may no longer be as rowdy as it once was, but you'll still find strangers flirting in the garden, letting loose to live music or maybe even daring to sample snacks from The Dolphin's fairly new pizzeria. Let's hope the pub doesn't embrace any other new-fangled ideas and stays as it is, oblivious to the area's trends.

Address 163a Mare Street, E8 3RH, +44 (0)20 8985 3727, www.facebook.com/
dolphinhackney | **Getting there** London Fields (Overground) | **Hours** Mon–Thu
4pm–2am, Fri & Sat 3pm–4am, Sun 4pm–2am | **Tip** To carry on partying even later, head
to nearby club Oval Space for regular raves into the wee hours.

30__Doodle Bar
Chalk good times up to this bar's arty USP

Some struggle with their words after a few too many shandies, but the punters at Doodle Bar don't have any trouble expressing themselves. Instead, this bar lets its patrons scrawl whatever the hell they like, wherever the hell they like. The Doodle Bar concept first came to life in Battersea in 2009 when a pop-up took over a riverside warehouse and allowed guests to scribble on every surface imaginable – even the waiting staff's whites. The idea was so popular that the bar became a permanent feature for a further six years. That was until the warehouse was sold off to make way for luxury flats; such is the way in London.

Luckily, the team found a space just as edgy for the concept to live on in 2016 – an inconspicuous railway arch in Bermondsey. This incarnation of Doodle Bar is still in its infancy, but it's already pulling in punters thanks to its fun USP and loyal followers prepared to stray from southwest London. They fill up the narrow room where two walls of the arch are covered with blackboards and chalk is available by the bucket-load.

Those who don't consider themselves a budding Picasso can sit back and soak up the graffiti action sipping one of the bar's original cocktails or the specially brewed Doodle craft lager. Hopefully it'll give them the Dutch courage to have a crack at scribbling in front of a fun-filled room. But if not, the works of 'art' on the walls will be entertainment enough (mostly of animals and their appendages). If your skill set is more sport-based, you can still get playful on one of the many ping-pong tables stretching back to the rear of the room. In fact, add to art and sport regular Spanish film nights and you've got most extracurricular activities covered. With all that going on, it's well worth fuelling up with street-food snacks – every weekend a different trader parks its van out in front of this party arch for hungry hipsters to get grazing.

Address 60 Druid Street, SE1 2EZ, +44 (0)20 7403 3222, www.thedoodlebar.com, reservations@thedoodlebar.com | Getting there Bermondsey (Jubilee Line, Overground) | Hours Thu noon–11pm, Fri & Sat noon–midnight, Sun noon–6pm | Tip There's even more street-food wonder in the area if you visit at weekends and take a trip down the buzzing Maltby Street Market.

31 Dovetail

Mecca for Belgian beer lovers

While there's a lot to be said for the buzzing beer hall vibe of the more famous Dove pub along Hackney's Broadway Market, it is sister bar Dovetail hidden down Clerkenwell's Jerusalem Passage that comes recommended for a quality Belgian beer fix in London. It has just as much of a mind-blowing line-up of beers – from pilsners to gueuzes to blondes – as the bigger east London boozer, yet offers a way more appealing continental character.

This authentic feel may come from brown stone floor tiles, the kind of bulky wooden tables that can endure a solid drinking session and fetching white-tiled walls, which cut an even prettier line towards the rear of the room where they contrast starkly with chairs backed by wooden arches. These give an almost monastic quality the Trappists would approve of. They'd probably also enjoy the grub, which does just as roaring a trade at lunchtime as it does in the evenings. Steaming bowls of moules frites are the most popular, but beef carbonnade and Belgian croquettes are other faithful flavours worth seeking out. Or stick with a popular gourmet burger to complement your suds.

And really, it's all about the best Belgian beer you'll find in London, a pioneering line-up of over 100 options by the bottle and around ten on draught to sample too. If you're unsure about where to begin with such a wide selection, try one of the bar's tasting events for guidance from beer sommeliers (yes, that's a job!). Or if you think you already know your hops from a hole in the ground, test your prowess at a pub quiz that throws in the odd obligatory beer-related question.

You'll pay a premium for sipping such rare finds in the UK, but it's worth it. While the Dove plays it safe with some international beers, Dovetail stays exclusively devoted to Belgium. You'll even find a few jenevers if you truly want to drink like the Belgians do.

Address 9–10 Jerusalem Passage, EC1V 4JP, +44 (0)20 7490 7321, www.dovepubs.com, dovetail@dovepubs.com | **Getting there** Farringdon (National Rail, Circle, Hammersmith & City, Metropolitan Lines) | **Hours** Mon–Sat noon–11pm | **Tip** For further continental exploration, head to nearby Dans Le Noir, a French restaurant where you dine in pitch darkness.

32 Drapers Arms
Officially London's best Scotch egg

The gastropub trend first took off in London in 1995 when The Eagle landed in Farringdon. Tucking into seared scallops and pork belly in relaxed surrounds any night of the week became the norm as gastropubs spread like butterflied chicken. While the UK is now littered with gentrified pubs that put on the airs and graces for the *Michelin Good Pub Guide*-wielding masses, you'll still find some of the more authentic foodie pubs in London. The Drapers Arms earns its stripes – a restaurant with connections and influential fans it may be, but it's also got heaps of pub substance.

Its baby-blue exterior is a little arresting on the backstreets of almost-provincial Barnsbury. But inside this Georgian building, walls are a muted mint green, with warped floorboards adding rustic charm and chunky tables circling a horseshoe bar. A classy dining room sits on the first floor while a spacious beer garden at the rear is a place for Islington's hound brigade to socialise. A wall of shelves is given up to an astonishing collection of Penguin Classics and a stash of board games includes bespoke jigsaw puzzles made from photos of the pub.

Salsify, sorrel and samphire are just some of the Waitrose ingredients on the posh gastropub menu, with head chef Gina Hopkins cooking up a storm. Prices are steep, but it's worth it. And if you're not here for a slap-up meal, at the very least order classic pub snacks at the bar; the Drapers is a three-time winner of London's annual Scotch Egg Challenge despite fierce competition.

So what about those connections? In 2009, the Drapers Arms reopened under business partners Nick Gibson and Ben Maschler, son of renowned *Guardian* food critic Faye Maschler. And the pub's fame in foodie circles remains, with up-and-coming London chefs Elizabeth Haigh and Neil Rankin known to Instagram their Sunday sessions. You're in good company.

Address 44 Barnsbury Street, N1 1ER, +44 (0)20 7619 0348, www.thedrapersarms.com, info@thedrapersarms.com | Getting there Highbury & Islington (Victoria Line, Overground) | Hours Daily noon–11pm | Tip In Islington, you're never far from a gastropub. If you can't get a table at the Drapers, head to Smokehouse on Canonbury Road or the Pig and Butcher on Liverpool Road.

33___Drink, Shop & Do
All your favourite things under one roof

For once, the name says a lot. Drinking comes in the form of original tea blends by day and Prosecco-based cocktails by night at King's Cross' quirky Drink, Shop & Do. The all-day and late-night joint is a stylish blend of bar, café, shop, disco and village hall (or as close to one as you can get in the capital). The split-level venue fills the space of what was a Turkish bathhouse in the Victorian era and a haven for illegal raves in the '80s. That's not the only naughtiness though; up until recently, an erotica store was found in the basement, and Drink, Shop & Do still makes a nod and a wink to the fact with cheeky neon signs advertising elicit activities. Don't worry, they just use the basement as a dance floor now.

The shopping element may not be the first thing you notice. The beautiful, tall-ceilinged café upstairs is always prettily dressed with ever-changing pastel-coloured craft creations – from bunting to pom poms – made on site by visitors. It sure makes a sweet setting for a glitter-filled afternoon tea or twee hen do. But other elements of the décor can change from week to week, with all furniture discreetly priced up for sale. As one employee puts it, 'You can buy everything, except the staff'. It's way more fun than an eBay auction, and littered around the place are trinkets, stationery and homeware for sale, too.

So what about the 'Dos'? They're as creative as the rest of the venue, with a choc-a-block timetable of one-off and regular events including quirky craft sessions (from nipple tassle making to adult colouring-in), skill shops (from calligraphy to learning to bounce like Beyoncé) and wild nights out (from beer pong to bingo fronted by a cast of drag queens). This is the heartland of the operation, where founders and school friends Coralie Sleap and Kristie Bishop knew there'd be an interest in friends coming together for a stitch and bitch, and then a boogie.

Address 9 Caledonian Road, N1 9DX, +44 (0)20 7278 4335, www.drinkshopdo.co.uk, mail@drinkshopdo.co.uk | **Getting there** King's Cross St Pancras (Circle, Hammersmith & City, Metropolitan, Northern, Piccadilly, Victoria Lines, National Rail) | **Hours** Mon – Thu 10.30am – midnight, Fri & Sat 10.30am – 2am, Sun 10.30am – 8pm | **Tip** Carry on the movement at Frame, a dance and fitness studio with modern rave and barre classes.

34 Earl of Essex

Say a little prayer for brew

The most famous man to hold the title of Earl of Essex has to be Henry VIII's advisor Thomas Cromwell. His family ran a brewery and owned a tavern, with his father being reported to the courts for watering down the beer in his establishment. That wouldn't have gone down well with fans of this Earl of Essex, a temple to beer down an Islington street filled with dreamy townhouses. As you enter the pretty teal-paint and brown-tile pub there's a dominatingly large wooden hymn board to your left, upon which the day's drinks pouring at the bar are listed as gospel. Rightly so – this is Islington's first brewpub with grand stills tucked neatly behind the bar, all shiny and silver. A spot of beer reverence is expected.

What was once a Georgian pub decked in red and white and bearing England flags like an advert for UKIP reopened in July 2012 described as the sister pub to the King's Arms in Bethnal Green, a similarly beery hostelry (although it's a part of the Barworks group, who operate many great establishments in the capital). A utilitarian look and Shaker-style furnishings complete the holy hops vibe. Seating in the gorgeously peaceful beer garden is in as much demand as the staff at the bar. Its modern bunting and potted plants make a match for the stylish interior, where bold framed prints by contemporary artists give an edge to beer evangelism.

And as for that beer board (which is regularly posted to Twitter to lure in the keenest hopheads), there are always over ten keg beers and a handful of options by cask from the likes of Thornbridge, Siren, Weird Beard and Magic Rock with closer-to-home flavours from Kernel, Five Points and Camden Town Brewery, some of them so strong, they're only served in half-pint measures. Wait for service from the aquamarine bar and it's sure to come with recommendations, just like the ones on the food menu, which pairs tipples with small plates. Basically, have full faith in finding a higher state of beer consciousness.

Address 25 Danbury Street, N1 8LE, +44 (0)20 7424 5828, www.earlofessex.net, earl@earlofessex.net | Getting there Angel (Northern Line) | Hours Mon–Thu noon–11.30pm, Fri & Sat noon–midnight, Sun noon–11pm | Tip The Duke of Cambridge pub at the other end of Danbury Street is as dedicated to organic food as the Essex is to beer. Go for gastropub goodness.

35 _ Effra Hall Tavern
Jerk chicken, jazz and very good vibes

On any given night, Caribbean boys sit at the bar dressed in trilby hats and tracksuits, overlooked by a clock in the shape of Jamaica. They chew the cud as if they're life-long friends, but it's feasible that they only just met, such is the camaraderie at Kellett Road's Effra Hall Tavern.

Brixton's Afro-Caribbean community is losing familiar social spaces as the pace of change in the area shifts a gear and upstart restaurants shuffle in to satisfy new kids on the block. But the Effra Hall Tavern stays true to the locals who have shaped this part of town more than any bout of gentrification. It serves up a fiery menu of Caribbean classics from plantain chips, jerk chicken and a mean lamb curry to transmogrified takes on British pub grub – Red Stripe-battered cod and chips, for example. Every Tuesday a band called the Soothsayers sets up in the corner to play reggae-influenced tunes, while Sundays have seen open jazz jam nights led by local soul diva Lauren Dalrymple for over 20 years. At quieter times, you may even spot generations slamming down the dominoes, although that's less common these days.

None of it is to the exclusion of other locals. All are welcome to take comfort in a stripped-back setting where an old brass-and-wood bar sweeps both sides of the room, rustic chairs are fashioned from chunky blocks of wood and dune-coloured curtains dress the windows. And some pub staples are kept resolutely intact, with football shown on projector screens and in the palm-lined beer garden. Admirably cheap pints include local Brixton Brewery's Effra lager. Both this and the pub take their name from the area's River Effra, one of the capital's 'lost rivers' forced below ground to form part of the Victorian infrastructure. In some ways, you can draw comparisons between the Effra and this counterculture backstreet pub, a hidden wonder to those aware of its existence.

Address 38 Kellett Road, SW2 1EB, +44 (0)20 7274 4180, www.theeffra.com |
Getting there Brixton (Victoria Line) | **Hours** Mon–Wed noon–11.30pm, Thu–Sat
noon–midnight, Sun noon–11pm | **Tip** Brixton's Club 414 and The Prince of Wales are
two more local spots for great live jazz nights.

36 — The Eight Bells

Football, food and old-school Fulham

If you asked a tourist to paint a picture of a Great British Pub, it would probably look like The Eight Bells. Enthusiastic drinkers line the pavement on picnic benches out front or find shelter under the building's bottle-green awnings. Inside, a single room is filled with chatter and clinking glasses as groups gather round pints and packets of crisps torn open and laid flat on the table for sharing (pub salad, anyone?). A semi-circular bar stands in the middle, the heart of the room. Well, unless Chelsea or Fulham are playing, in which case TV screens command all attention. A blackboard presents the kind of comforting pub grub that fuels this nation – gammon, egg and chips, scampi, bangers and mash, steak and ale pie. Friday lunchtimes are heaving, showing that some traditions will never die. Much like the pub's red patterned carpet.

It's a stark contrast to an end of the High Street that doesn't feel buzzy at all. This road became a cul-de-sac in 1886, when what was then known as the Fulham Bridge was rebuilt to become Putney Bridge, diverting traffic away from the High Street. As a consequence, the pub received compensation for loss of trade. You'd hardly know it now, especially on match days when Craven Cottage spectators pile in for pre-match beers. Although you're more likely to find away supporters in the Eight Bells, since the pub pledges its allegiance to Chelsea FC, with staff in their blues on Soccer Saturdays. You may find the odd animal in football strip as well, with two pub cats and two pub dogs, the pugs named Steven Gerrard (odd) and Chelsea (more fitting).

It's right that the local teams sit at the heart of the Eight Bells. The Putney Bridge pub was used as a temporary changing room for Fulham Football Club from 1886 to 1888 when their grounds were based at Ranelagh House, even closer to the Bells. It's fair to say footie is in this pub's DNA.

Address 89 Fulham High Street, SW6 3JS, +44 (0)20 7736 6307, www.facebook.com/eightbellsfulham | Getting there Putney Bridge (District Line) | Hours Mon–Wed 10am–11.30pm, Thu–Sat 10am–midnight, Sun 10am–11.30pm | Tip Hurlingham Books at the top of the High Street is another dreamy tourist spot, a second-hand shop from 1968.

37 Elephant & Castle

From rave to new wave drinking

Inside these four walls it comes as a surprise that this exact spot has seen so much history. It's a little slice of modernity on the surface, having reopened fairly recently with a new look from the prolific Antic pub chain. The group has opted for low lighting, long red-velvet banquettes and an open-plan layout, keeping large windows with a view out to the clattering comings and goings of Elephant & Castle's busy junction. You can hardly imagine horses and carts rolling past in the good old days, but this is the site of the former coaching inn that gave the entire area its name, with first records of it dating back as far as 1765.

Even more interesting is this pub's modern and somewhat chequered history. In the '90s, its daytime parties were where Saturday clubbers carried on from the night before. Many cite it as the birthplace of UK garage with DJ Matt Jam Lamont's 'Happy Days' raves leading the charge. But the fun had to stop in 2015 when an unfortunate punter was jabbed in the eye with a pen. Not all is fair in love and rave and as such, the pub had its licence revoked. And as with all London pubs, it wasn't long before developers were sniffing around this prime location.

'Prime location' is the operative term, since Foxtons estate agents were the ones eyeing up (ahem) the space for their next branch. In an area where social housing had already made way for luxury flats, the further threat of gentrification saw a group of squatters move in, covering the pub in tasteful 'Fuck Foxtons' graffiti. They were evicted after a month's occupation but their statement seemed to work, as the Elephant & Castle was deemed an asset of community value and the pub was saved. From all those fairy lights, craft beers and gastropub dishes, you'd never know such recent conflict had taken place right here. The days of rave may be in the past, but a new era of hip drinking has been ushered in.

Address 119 Newington Causeway, SE1 6BN, +44 (0)20 7403 8124, www.elephantandcastlepub.com | **Getting there** Elephant & Castle (Bakerloo, Northern Lines, National Rail) | **Hours** Mon–Thu 4pm–midnight, Fri 4pm–2am, Sat & Sun noon–midnight | **Tip** UK garage lives on in the area. Check out long-standing superclub Ministry of Sound or, better still, head to nearby Corsica Studios for label-pushing beats.

38_Evans & Peel Detective Agency

Undercover drinking that's far from elementary

In a city full of speakeasies, what's a bar got to do to stand out? That's one case that Evans & Peel Detective Agency has cracked by going all-out with its secretive film-noir style. When it opened in 2012, it was yet another treatment of the speakeasy theme that was spreading around London like illegal hooch in Prohibition America. But this bar has stood the test of time.

The premise is simple: present your case to the undercover detective agency (specialists in 'blackmail, missing persons and armed personal protection'). Yet the delivery is anything but. Fill in a case file on the agency's website to make an appointment and upon arrival, press the buzzer at an office door lit by one lonely lamp overhead. You'll be summoned to a moody, green bureau with notes and newspaper clippings in among magnifying glasses and other sneaky secret paraphernalia. The only clue that something more is afoot is the hum of chatter nearby. A sassy detective will enquire about your case before pulling back a bookcase, and as if by magic you'll be transported to a barely-lit 1920s bar.

The black-and-white-movie chic continues with waitresses carrying menus in brown paper folders. But otherwise, the Prohibition theme prevails over undercover antics. Bottles of grog – or beer and champagne – are delivered in brown paper bags while the house beer is served as moonshine decanted from an old radiator. The room fully looks the part, with chairs made from old Singer sewing machine parts, the bar made from church pews and a set of drawers behind sourced from a library, where regular 'clients' can keep a bottle of their favourite grog. Visitors make the effort too, with some donning flapper dresses or braces and flat caps for a guaranteed big night out. Case closed.

Address 310c Earls Court Road, SW5 9BA, www.evansandpeel.com | **Getting there** Earls Court (Circle, District, Piccadilly Lines) | **Hours** Tue–Fri 5pm–midnight, Sat 5pm–12.30am | **Tip** If immersive is your thing, try the escape games by Do Stuff, also in southwest London at South West Eleven near Battersea Park.

39__FAM Bar
Yes, fam!

London is a city full of slang, but one of the phrases of the day is 'fam': a term used to greet those you consider as close as family. That warmth is worn well by a bar of the same name, which opened its doors at the end of 2018. It's not a family-run operation, but it champions 'chosen family' by placing pictures of friends in frames. Indeed, FAM's fam takes up an entire wall of this bijou room, with many smiling faces from the international drinks industry included.

The founding team is composed of Megs Miller, a tequila ambassador from Canada, her partner Rhys Wilson and cocktail industry pro Dre Masso – Miller was the first person Masso hired as a bartender when he launched Opium in 2012 (ch. 70). You have Miller to thank for the cosy feel of FAM, as she designed the place, picking up second-hand materials from an antiques market to tie in with the bar's sustainable ethos. She and Wilson used to live in Colombia, and warm splashes of colour show the country's influence on the pair. Adding even more vibrancy is another wall that's dedicated to vinyl – team members have chosen their favourite records, and punters can pluck one from the rack and ask to put it on the player.

Cocktails are original drinks, many referencing the tracks from those LPs. But it's the FAM Margarita that's famous, the sharp Mexican cocktail smoothed out with Devon flower honey; it's a great example of how FAM champions local first in its quest for sustainability. See this approach also in homely food that breaks bar snack norms, from cups of soup to tortilla chips with the kind of sloppy cheese dip you could only really share with very close friends.

You'll often see mates chatting at the bar and sometimes with Miller and Wilson's dachshund Derek, too. This is living room drinking round the back of Oxford Street. Grab your own fam, hang up your coat like this is your home and get cosy on the cocktails.

Address 31 Duke Street, W1U 1LG, www.fam.bar, hello@fam.bar | Getting there Bond Street (Central, Jubilee Lines) | Hours Tue–Wed 4pm–midnight, Thu & Fri 4pm–1am, Sat 2pm–1am | Tip Sate any late-night cravings after FAM closes at nearby burger joint MeatLiquor on Margaret Street. They're open until 3am and there's a giant neon pickle inside helping to bring the party vibe.

40___Faltering Fullback

The best beer garden going

The petite entrance of this vine-clad pub is misleading to say the least. Not in a million years would you imagine it to be concealing a sprawling boozer with a tough rugger-loving crowd behind its doors. Nor would you know the Fullback is in possession of what must be London's finest beer garden.

A horseshoe bar in this former Courage pub (originally the Sir Walter Scott and dating back to 1874) spreads across two rooms to the front and left, where trinkets, musical instruments and drinking vessels dangle from the ceiling's wooden rafters. You can see it and all its quirks in Slow Club's music video for 'Beginners' in which Daniel Radcliffe rambles round the light-filled rooms with only empty pint glasses for company (it's odd to see the place so quiet). To the right is a large beer hall with picnic benches, which are prettied with posies in jars. Flowers don't really do the job, but people are more engaged in a group celebration, a game of pool on a table to the rear or the rugby, football or large sporting events shown about the room on TV screens up high. Rugby takes precedence.

Cheap pints fly around, as do nourishing bowls of Thai curry from the kitchen. Service won't necessarily come with a smile but that's of little concern when you discover the Fullback's behemoth of a beer garden. It spans several floors, with decking draped in twisted foliage and concealing enough nooks and crannies for it to feel like the Ewok village from *Return of the Jedi*.

Back inside, you may find the odd green-and-orange souvenir giving away that this is actually an Irish pub. There are occasional folk-music nights, but otherwise the agenda is geared towards having good old-fashioned fun regardless of whether your ties are Celtic. Find a weekly pub quiz, an open-mic night or punters just enjoying the surprising buzz of this permanently heaving place, indoors and out.

Address 19 Perth Road, N4 3HB, +44 (0)20 7272 5834, www.falteringfullback.com | **Getting there** Finsbury Park (Piccadilly, Victoria Lines) | **Hours** Mon–Thu noon–midnight, Fri & Sat noon–1am, Sun noon–11.30pm | **Tip** Find a different kind of sporting action at Rowans Tenpin Bowl on Stroud Green Road, open late and serving alcoholic slushies.

41　First Aid Box

Just what the doctor ordered

A suite of scalpels spreads across a metallic trolley, a book by St John's Ambulance perches on the windowsill and stethoscopes dangle from lamps, all part of a hospital-meets-science-lab theme. But that shouldn't be too shocking, since Herne Hill's neighbourhood bar calls itself First Aid Box. It's a petite room with a clinical feel from shiny white wall tiles, but the rest is pure silliness – particularly the drink menus kept safe in plastic folders like worksheets from biology class. There's no Bunsen burner on your table, but a blowtorch is in operation at the bar.

Drinks are put together at a workstation in the middle of the room and fall under two categories: 'Doctor's Orders' and 'Against Doctor's Orders'. The former reads like Deliciously Ella's idea of a cocktail list, using superfoods from blueberries to unconventional quinoa. The latter list is much more loose, with sinful drinking on the agenda. Sip from an intravenous bag filled with syrupy, sweet punch or order the 'Coffee and Cigarettes', a twist on a classic espresso martini with added smoke from the burning embers of an orange on the side. It's as theatrical as the operating table. If you're unconvinced by the medical stunts, a secretive bar-within-a-bar called Blinder sits at the rear and channels some serious Victoriana. Named after gritty interwar drama *Peaky Blinders*, it's a dimly-lit, spit-and-sawdust speakeasy with a lean towards whisky.

Owners Dave Tregenza and Chris Edwards crossed paths on the Canary Wharf bar scene and sparked off each other's creativity in a part of town where it's perhaps a little lacking. They established their own drink consultancy and opened Brixton bars Shrub & Shutter in 2014 and First Aid Box at the end of 2015. So the next time you're in need of imaginative cocktails, maybe you won't have to venture all the way into Zone 1. First Aid Box is the cure for what ails you.

Address 119 Dulwich Road, Herne Hill, SE24 0NG, +44 (0)20 7274 6409, www.firstaidbox2015.com, info@firstaidbox2015.com | Getting there Brixton (Victoria Line) | Hours Tue–Thu 5–11pm, Fri 5pm–midnight, Sat 9am–midnight | Tip Coffee that's not in cocktail form – the Lido Café just over the road is a huge hit for summer brunch by the swimming pool.

42__The Four Quarters
Get your geek on

Proof that computer games aren't just for kids, The Four Quarters in Peckham combines sipping craft beer with shooting bad guys and tearing round racetracks. The bar is modelled on a formula popular in the US, with arcade games operated by the quarter dollar. Here, they take your pound coins at the bar and convert them to quarters from a retro machine on the wall, leaving you free to get gaming.

The Four Quarters opened in the summer of 2014, but owners Joe Dowling and Tom Humphrey had form in London's gaming scene, running their own shop, Retro Game Base, in Streatham (where punters could pick up Sega, SNK and Playstation classics). The minimal space pairs harsh concrete floors with battered, reclaimed furniture, but if you're pulling up a seat, you're missing the point. All the games are restored relics, including incredibly rare and mint condition machines. Punters vie for high scores on classics like *Pac-Man* and *Street Fighter II* while the more seasoned players gather round *Asteroids*. Console games are projected so you can catch all the *Golden Eye* action on the wall.

Tournaments and parties are advertised thick and fast on the bar's Twitter page. The nostalgia factor is also aided by '80s and '90s movie nights, while nerds of a different kind flock in for dubstep and drum-and-bass label parties (when 8-bit tracks aren't the only thing filling the air). Drinks are locally crafted beers and quirky cocktails, and like any decent bar in London, a secret basement bar, The Confession Room, lies in wait towards the weekend.

While many other bars and arcades of this ilk cropped up across the capital around the same time, The Four Quarters is the only one with enough appeal to warrant a second branch, which opened in Hackney Wick in 2017. It's great, for once, to see London drinkers glued to a screen other than the one on their smartphone.

Address 187 Rye Lane, SE15 4TP, +44 (0)20 3754 7622, www.facebook.com/
fourquartersbar | **Getting there** Peckham Rye (National Rail, Overground) | **Hours**
Mon–Wed 5.30pm–1am, Thu 5.30pm–1.30am, Fri 5pm–2am, Sat 1pm–2am, Sun
3.30–11pm | **Tip** For more playfulness in Peckham, check out Canavan's Pool Hall
down the road: functioning pool hall and bar by day, fully-fledged nightclub by night.

43__Four Thieves

Let the games begin

The decline of the Great British boozer: a worrying trend, with UK pubs closing at a rate of 21 a week. As homes gain games consoles and as supermarkets offer increasingly sophisticated drinks, the big night out down the local may soon be a thing of the past. That's unlikely to ever be the case at Battersea's Four Thieves, a multi-roomed bonanza where there's a queue on the door on Saturdays. Here, they're raising the game – literally.

At the Four Thieves you'll find all kinds of entertainment you simply can't get from your sofa. The pub stocks Laine's beers available at the chain's other London pubs, as well as a one-off ESB brewed on site. To keep up with burgeoning booze trends, it also distils a gin best sipped in summer in the pub's gin yard. Fashions in food are covered too, with the likes of tacos and Korean wings on the menu.

Then there's the entertainment spread over several rooms. The Four Thieves hosts an immersive escape game called Lady Chastity's Reserve, a crazy golf course and a retro RC racetrack in its ever-popular arcade room (where you'll also find *Time Crisis II*, *Sega Rally* and *Tekken* on a big screen). Meanwhile, the Boat Room – where drinks are served from a bar fashioned from an old sailing vessel – has more old-school entertainment from pub quizzes to stand-up. You may even receive banter at the bar, where quick-witted staff are the ones jostling for your attention.

Slightly less upbeat are the pub's plague references. The Lavender Hill local takes its name from a group of medieval grave-robbers who were spared their lives in return for the powers that stopped them contracting the Black Death. It turns out they were dousing themselves in lavender oil, a lesser-known flea repellent. Although a poster depicting the ring of roses makes reference to the tale, it's the cheeky nature of those Four Thieves that's been honoured best at this fun-time pub.

Address 51 Lavender Gardens, SW11 1DJ, +44 (0)20 7223 6927, www.fourthieves.pub, hello@fourthieves.pub | **Getting there** Clapham Junction (Overground, National Rail) | **Hours** Mon–Thu noon–midnight, Fri & Sat noon–2am, Sun noon–10.30pm | **Tip** For traditional arts and entertainment, Battersea Arts Centre has it all in a stunning Art Deco space. The grand hall burnt down in 2015 but reopened to much fanfare in 2018.

44_Fourpure Basecamp

A landmark on London's beeriest stretch

Many of London's streets are flowing with booze, but one in particular is known for its strong ties with the hop stuff. This stretch just south of London Bridge and down towards South Bermondsey has become affectionately known as the Bermondsey Beer Mile (although it has sprawled to more than a mile by now). The area's industrial estates and railway arches have lent themselves especially well to a microbrewing trend that swept the capital. The Kernel was the first brewery to plant a flag in one of the warehouse spaces here in 2009, and by 2013, Fourpure Brewing Company had joined the gang – setting up shop with a brewery and taproom at the southernmost point and, as such, marking the start or finish of a Beer Mile bar crawl.

Established by two young brothers Dan and Tom Lowe, Fourpure and its sessionable range of IPAs rapidly grew in popularity, and investment from a large Aussie drink firm (a trend that's rife in craft beer right now) later followed. The money might have meant big things for the company and its beery output, but it has also had a big impact on Bermondsey's bar-crawlers.

In July 2019, Fourpure relaunched its attached taproom, making it one of the most accomplished along the Beer Mile. The space has a mezzanine level overlooking a bright-orange horseshoe bar, behind which there are 43 taps to choose from, showcasing the Fourpure range as well as stuff from fellow brewers. Plants drape themselves around the space as they do in any millennial Londoner's living room, cocoon chairs swing from the ceiling and plenty of hopheads and stag do goers mill about. There's room for 400 of them here.

They've renamed the taproom 'Basecamp', which may speak of the brewery's ambitions. But to many, it's all about an inviting start-point ahead of a great beery expedition; one taproom so filled with liquid delights, you may never want to set off to the next one.

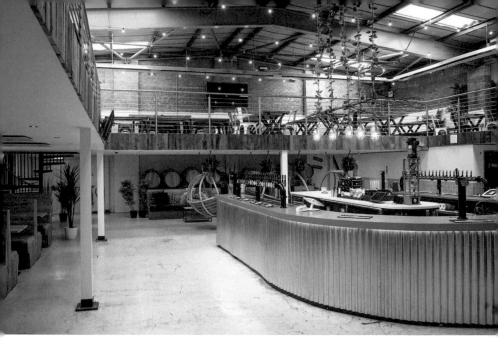

Address Bermondsey Trading Estate, 22 Rotherhithe New Road, SE16 3LL, +44 (0)20 3744 2141, www.fourpure.com, info@fourpure.com | **Getting there** South Bermondsey (National Rail) | **Hours** Tue noon–8pm, Wed-Fri noon–10pm, Sat 11am–8pm, Sun noon–8pm | **Tip** Continue up the Bermondsey Beer Mile for more breweries than you can shake a beer tasting paddle at – or swing by Hawkes Cidery, an appely anomaly along the sudsy stretch.

45 Frank's Café

Campari on the roof of a Peckham car park

If you go to one bar and one bar only south of the river, make it Frank's. Visiting the rooftop spot on the top of a Peckham car park has become something of a rite of passage for in-the-know Londoners who flock here come summer for Campari-based cocktails as the sun descends behind a vast urban skyline.

But there's way more to Frank's Café than a hip location, a cool crowd and a stonking view. The car park upon which it sits is a bit of a cultural institution. Art movement Bold Tendencies took over the space in 2007, a year later setting up Frank's on the roof. Every year, Bold Tendencies commissions brand-new artistic and musical installations for the space. As such, you may find an orchestra playing in among hay bales, or squiggly silver lines covering the floor like a giant snail trail. In fact, the iconic, ship-like structure made from dark wood and red tarpaulin that shelters the bar itself is a work by, among others, Paloma Gormley, the daughter of famous sculptor Antony Gormley.

It seems it's all about pedigree here. The eponymous Frank is part of the Boxer family. His grandmother Arabella was a pioneering food writer, his father, Charlie, owns cult deli Italo in Vauxhall and his brother, Jackson, runs popular Brunswick House Café, also in Vauxhall. Frank turned his hand to a menu of Italian aperitifs long before anyone else in the capital had embraced the red-booze trend. He professes to be quite partial to an Americano himself, but the Aperol Spritz is probably the most popular drink. The accompanying food line-up changes annually, but expect forward-thinking Italian flavours cooked on a barbecue grill.

Granted, during those rare London heatwaves you'll have a queue on your hands, both on the door and at the bar. But from one pilgrimage to Peckham it's easy to see why other cities around the world have started to motor on with the car park bar trend.

Address 10th Floor, Peckham Multi-Storey Car Park, 95A Rye Lane, SE15 4ST, www.frankscafe.org.uk, info@frankscafe.org.uk | Getting there Peckham Rye Station (National Rail, Overground) | Hours May–Oct only: Tue–Fri 5–11pm, Sat & Sun 11am–11pm | Tip If the queue is too long on a sunny trip to Frank's, try the nearby Bussey Building for its rooftop film club instead.

46__ The French House
Writers, thinkers and old-school drinkers

There's no way you can talk of Soho without mentioning The French House. It's one of the few bastions of the area's fading bohemia, and while drinking in here these days probably won't offer such chance encounters with poets, artists and bon vivants, you can still hear history echoing in the pub's timber walls and catch a glimpse of it in faded black-and-white photos.

It's gone under many names, such as Victor Berlemont and The York Minster, but its true patrons only ever refer to it as 'The French'. But it's a case of false identity, with former landlords Victor Berlemont and son Gaston (his curly moustache as famous as his pub) hailing from Belgium. The Berlemont line took over the pub around the time of World War I and it became a favoured base for the Free French during World War II, even hosting Charles de Gaulle for a glass of wine (although widespread rumours that he wrote his famous rallying speech here are thought to be untrue).

The pub was a focal point for Soho's Post-War hedonism, attracting writers and poets (Sylvia Plath signed a book deal over drinks while Dylan Thomas temporarily lost his *Under Milk Wood* manuscript after a session), artists (Francis Bacon, Lucian Freud), thinkers (John Mortimer) and drinkers (Jeffrey Bernard). Whatever their persuasion, they were welcome for many bevvies and – above all else – titillating conversation.

Still insanely popular, you'll now find media types on the pavement underneath the tricolour, half pints in hand (with pints only served on April Fool's Day at the pub's annual fundraiser). The upstairs room has even been home to some of the best restaurant residencies (St John and Polpetto). Older generations still cosy up indoors over Ricard and wine, staying loyal to the no-mobile-phone rule. So, even if the times have changed, The French is still an institution and a looking glass to Soho's past. Vive la France!

Address 49 Dean Street, W1D 5BG, +44 (0)20 7437 2477, www.frenchhousesoho.com | Getting there Leicester Square (Northern, Piccadilly Lines) | Hours Mon–Sat noon–11pm, Sun noon–10.30pm | Tip For more French style in Soho, take a trip to Maison Bertaux on Greek Street. It declares itself to be London's oldest patisserie and is famed for its Dijon slice.

47__ The George
A scenic haunt of Shakespearian significance

While Borough Market is the place where foodies flock, The George is what brings pub aficionados from all around the world to Southwark. That includes names as big as Beyoncé, and it's because you probably won't find a London pub with more history. It's got so much to say for itself, renowned beer writer Pete Brown has dedicated a whole book to it. And it means so much to English history that the National Trust bought the pub in 1937.

You feel the history as you enter under the arched gateway into a cobbled yard surrounded by ancient balconies. It's London's only surviving galleried coaching inn, its current look lingering from the Stuart era when it was rebuilt after the Great Fire of London. But the George has actually been around since the 1500s, and the courtyard in which it resides since as far back as the 1300s. Indeed, Geoffrey Chaucer's 1383 chronicle *The Canterbury Tales* began in the Tabard Inn, a pub that shared this very site until it was demolished in the 1870s. Like in Chaucer's tale, many began their southbound pilgrimage here, giving the pub a semi-holy status. But in actual fact, this and the Tabard were two of eight great coaching inns outside the city's barriers and known for medieval lawlessness.

It was the kind of scene that lured in Samuel Pepys – who documented bare-knuckle fights and prostitution – as well as William Shakespeare. As the playwright's star took off, he didn't lose a connection with the Southwark inn that he used to frequent, with the yard becoming a theatre for his plays, a temporary stage set up at the entrance and spectators occupying the galleries. Although parts of what was a sprawling mix of bedrooms, restaurants, bars and brothels have been sold off, the slice of The George that remains speaks of the atmospheric drinking of years gone by. When summer rolls around and punters crowd the pavement for an outdoor sports screening, you can almost imagine it.

Address 75–77 Borough High Street, SE1 1NH, +44 (0)20 7407 2056, www.george-southwark.co.uk, hello@george-southwark.co.uk | Getting there London Bridge (Jubilee, Northern Lines, National Rail) | Hours Mon–Sat 11am–11pm, Sun noon–9pm | Tip Visit nearby Southwark Cathedral to marvel at a memorial to Shakespeare, a three-window tribute in stained glass depicting famous scenes from his plays.

48__ The Glory
Living on the edge

The Glory doesn't need a rainbow flag to mark its entrance. This 'gender-upending, forward-thinking' drinker is stripped-back, cool and far from camp in its approach to LGBTQ+ culture. It opened to much fanfare in December 2014, since the names behind this operation hold serious clout on the queer scene. Most notably, there's Jonny Woo, drag artiste extraordinaire with twenty years of celebrity on his CV for mind-bending performance in theatre, comedy and cabaret. He and co-owner John Sizzle are probably best known for Gay Bingo, an entertainment night and cultural phenomenon that took London by storm for 13 years. The pair, along with two other founders, have made a home for counterculture entertainment at The Glory, with life drawing, lectures and lip-syncing competitions for drag queens and kings. They put on their own performances as well as holding an annual competition to crown the next Mr Glory. Expect the pub to also honour its heroes, with George Michael tribute nights and a Kate Bush cabaret.

This all sounds intense, but that's just the evening's entertainment. During the day, the pub is a relaxed and welcoming joint decorated in blue and serving quality cocktails. The team spent three years trying to find the dream spot and it's clear they've chosen well at the foot of Dalston's thriving nightlife scene. It's all done with an east London edge, celebrating alternative cabaret culture away from the clichés.

It's a vibe that's earned The Glory its fair share of famous fans – fashion's Christopher Kane, comedy's Simon Amstel, and pop music's Boy George and Peaches – as well as allowing the pub to spread across the UK as it tours to Glastonbury's queer club NYC Downlow, hosts mixed revues at Latitude festival, and takes to the stage at the National Theatre. But it's the real thing that counts; this Haggerston pub is the ultimate belle of the ball.

Address 281 Kingsland Road, E2 8AS, www.theglory.co, info@theglory.co | **Getting there** Haggerston (Overground) | **Hours** Mon–Thu 5pm–midnight, Fri & Sat 5pm–2am, Sun 1–11pm | **Tip** Carry on partying at Bethnal Green Working Men's Club, a similarly glitzy stage for alternative entertainment.

49__Golden Heart
…and a golden landlady

'Esquilant' is scrawled in pink neon by the door, telling you a lot about this Spitalfields drinking spot. The Golden Heart was something of a social hub for the Brit Art movement of the '90s and '00s, with landlady Sandra Esquilant named the 80th most influential person in the creative world by *Art Review* in 2002. It seems unlikely from the retro combination of striped wallpaper, stained glass, wooden framed bar and vintage jukebox. But this scribbling in the window is by Tracey Emin, given to the pub in honour of the landlady's 25th year at the helm.

It all happened for the Golden Heart in the '90s when local London art heroes Gilbert & George paid the pub a visit and were charmed by East End traditions (who doesn't love a pie-eating contest?) and colourful locals, from wheeler-dealers to nuns from the nearby Sisters of Mercy chapel. It was at a time when Sandra and her late husband Dennis were struggling. Spitalfields Market across the road and the Truman Brewery round the corner – the biggest brewery in the world at one time, who had established and designed the pub – had shut down in the '80s, and the days of trade through the door from 6am were gone. But influential pals joined Gilbert & George and the Golden Heart saw a change in fortune. Everyone from Jake and Dinos Chapman and Rebecca Warren to Kate Moss and Pete Doherty were spotted at a pub that had become the toast of the Brit Art world, with Emin becoming a firm friend of the pub.

People love or hate the often-brusque service, but those lucky enough to stop by in the days of Sandra hula-hooping on the bar know she's a landlady to cherish. Nowadays, it's more about modern art mingling with photos of Lady Di, peculiar locals and a young crowd of post-work drinkers. Soaring rents may have driven out Shoreditch's budding artists, but the hedonism that came with them will never leave.

Address 110 Commercial Street, E1 6LZ, +44 (0)20 7247 2158 | Getting there
Liverpool Street (Central, Circle, Hammersmith & City, Metropolitan Lines, National
Rail) | Hours Mon–Fri 11am–midnight, Sat 11–1am, Sun 11am–11pm | Tip Take
a stroll down to the Whitechapel Gallery for world-class modern art exhibitions along
with historic archives and collections.

50_Golden Lion

A roaring success

The landlords of a backstreet pub in Camden almost had the place bought from underneath them. The Golden Lion had been in the Murphy family for over 30 years when the lease of the pub came into question in 2011. Dave Murphy learned that the family's much-loved Lion had been sold to a mysterious private developer whose intentions to keep the place as a pub were ambiguous, to say the least. A long battle ensued over four years, until the Golden Lion was awarded back to its rightful owners. That a pub could almost be ripped from its landlords in the name of the city's rapid redevelopment is such a story of our times that *The Guardian* wrote extensively on the tale in its 'Long Read' section back in 2015.

After such a drawn-out struggle, it was hard for the Murphys to continue running the pub with the same passion as previous. But in 2018, they managed to breathe new life into the Golden Lion by partnering with two other publicans and former punters, Trevor Hunt and Aaron Carter. They've both brought with them expertise from years of service at other London pubs. Most notably, Hunt had done a four-year stint at the Drapers Arms (ch. 32) and so brought with him a bit of that foodie flair that the Islington gastropub is known for.

More space has been made for diners by removing the pub's pool table and fruit machines, but these tweaks haven't compromised the Golden Lion's good old-fashioned aesthetic or character. Stop by for one of the most affordable Sunday roasts in London (a plentiful plate of pub grub that doesn't scrimp on the trimmings) beside a glorious original bar saved from the boozer's Charrington Brewery days, and in among some proper Camden locals, from young dudes in trilby hats to pensioners who have a real rapport with bar staff. The Golden Lion is once again a great source of pride and joy for north Londoners.

Address 88 Royal College Street, NW1 0TH, +44 (0)20 7097 4760, www.goldenlioncamden.com | **Getting there** Camden Town (Northern Line) | **Hours** Mon–Sat noon–midnight, Sun noon–11pm | **Tip** Along the same street you'll find another handsome pub formerly run by Charrington Brewery, the Prince Albert, whose food menu is a bit more burger focused.

51__Gordon's Wine Bar

Cobwebs, candles and cases of the good stuff

Although London's oldest wine bar has been operated by a Gordon since 1890, it hasn't always been a case of keeping it in the family. It changed hands to a brand-new Gordon clan in the '70s, lured in by the name (they must have heard it was for sale through the grapevine). But Luis Gordon – already a sherry importer of some renown – was exactly the right kind of eccentric to take the reins at this cave of wine wonders.

For example, Luis' obituary in *The Times* in 2002 shared his love of driving an army tank or fire engine round his village in moments of quiet. This kind of madness extended to the running of Gordon's, where he insisted that cobwebs remain untouched when the venue closed for maintenance in the '90s. And even though he's no longer here to preside over the bar's rustic appeal, to this day Gordon's is run by the sherry buff's family and remains as he liked it: barely lit by old waxy candles, with damp bare stone competing with pleasant grapey aromas.

Gordon's Wine Bar has a history to match its ageing look. It's the cellars of Kipling House, where Rudyard Kipling once stayed and, dating even further back, where Samuel Pepys lived for a stint. And as for the past of the bar itself, it was established by the eponymous Angus Gordon in 1890 without any need for a licence. As one of the last remaining 'free vintners', Gordon was granted the power by a 1600's royal charter to sell wine to the public wherever he roamed (a privilege that has since been abolished).

As such, stars from Laurence Olivier to Vivien Leigh were drawn in by the dazzle of London's first continental-style wine bar. But these days, drinkers who populate Watergate Walk passageway outside in their droves don't seem to care much for all that, being more interested in bargain-bin ends and keeping a keen eye out for spare chairs and tables, as rare as a sighting of a 1945 Château Margaux.

Address 47 Villiers Street, WC2N 6NE, +44 (0)20 7930 1408, www.gordonswinebar.com, info@gordonswinebar.com | Getting there Embankment (Bakerloo, Circle, District, Northern Lines) | Hours Mon–Sat 11am–11pm, Sun noon–10pm | Tip Get better acquainted with the grape at nearby Terroris. The bar was pouring natural wine long before any of its trendier competitors.

52 The Grenadier

Meet Cedric at the Belgravia boo-zer

Play a game of spot the currency over pints once you find this diddy mews pub and former officers' mess in among the cobbled backstreets of Belgravia. The Grenadier has dollar bills, pound notes and money from around the world pinned to the ceiling and all along the walls. It was one officer in particular who earned the pub its impressive green display. A junior soldier known only as 'Cedric' is said to have met his end in the cellar one night in the 1770s, when a game of cards turned sour after the young foot guard couldn't pay the charge for cheating. His angry peers and opponents supposedly bludgeoned Cedric to death for his crimes. As such, tourists have taken it upon themselves to decorate the pub to help pay off the ill-fated grenadier's debt.

It just wouldn't be a London pub if a ghost story or two hadn't emerged from the sorry saga. From sightings of a lonely spectre to the sound of footsteps and sighs echoing up from the cellar, all have been reported, and staff and managers tell tales of broken glasses, moving furniture and even 'pokes'. This includes an account from a New Scotland Yard official claiming to have been burned on the hand by an invisible cigarette. It all sounds like nonsense, but take a visit to the Grenadier in winter months – even with the fire glowing, there's a distinct chill in the air that can only be described as otherworldly.

Ghost stories aside, the Grenadier has its other charms. Signs by the bar point to the 'Wellington Room' and the 'Boot Room' as if it's a sprawling maze of a pub but in actual fact, it could be one of London's smallest. The petite space is decorated with military costumes, paraphernalia and paintings, with the names and dates of battles plastered on the walls. These sit alongside framed newspaper clippings from around the world chronicling the sightings of Cedric, the pub's star attraction.

Address 18 Wilton Row, Belgrave Square, SW1X 7NR, +44 (0)20 7235 3074, www.taylor-walker.co.uk | Getting there Hyde Park Corner (Piccadilly Line) | Hours Daily noon–11pm | Tip Feeling inspired to see the queen's guards? Forego the tourists of Buckingham Palace in favour of spying on the foot guards at Wellington Barracks, where there's also a guard's museum.

53_Hacha

London's first agaveria

For many, the Mexican spirit mezcal – which, just like tequila, comes from distillation of the agave plant – is a lot to stomach. And all its variations can make it even more inaccessible to the outsider. But a visit to Hacha, London's very first 'agaveria', should take away the mysticism and ease you into mezcal loving. And that's probably in no small part because it's a labour of love, launched in 2019 by tequila ambassador and obsessive Deano Montcrieffe and his partner Emma Murphy.

The small room along Dalston's Kingsland Road feels larger than it should from its white brick walls and from light spilling into the room and bouncing off its surfaces. Beautiful, colourful tiles have been sourced directly from Mexico and are used as coasters for the cocktails. Rather than a flashy backbar, there's just one shelf of drinks, a well conceived row numbered one to 25 and labelled 'the agave list'. It's a regularly changing range of drinks made from the Oaxacan power plant, and includes mezcals and tequilas as well as the occasional sotol and raicilla for the more advanced enthusiast. There's also a small kitchen at the rear, which is filled by resident chefs with a South American lean to their cuisine.

You can choose to try any of the bottles from The Agave List by the glass or in a flight of three, with each paired with a snack – yes, they really do recommend things like chocolate and cheese to bring out the best of flavours from these strong spirits. Or try them in one of the bar's vibrant cocktails. Standouts include a champagne-laced take on the paloma or a tequila twist on the negroni. But it's the Mirror Margarita that's been turning heads: a see-through twist on Mexico's lynchpin mixed drink served from a piña-shaped drinks dispenser that sits on the bartop. It's now so popular, they've launched it in bottle form for punters to take home. It's truly dazzling stuff.

Address 378 Kingsland Road, E8 4AA, www.hachabar.com, hello@hachabar.com |
Getting there Dalston Junction (Overground Lines) | Hours Tue – Sat 5 – 11pm | Tip
The snacks at Hacha are solid, but for mind-blowing Mexican grub in London check out
Breddos Tacos on Goswell Road.

54__The Harp

Real beauty of a real-ale pub

To be the first London venue crowned Pub of the Year by CAMRA is not to be sniffed at. The organisation tends to champion bucolic inns in far-flung reaches of the UK where everyone's a friend you're yet to meet. But in 2011, the pub just a skip from Trafalgar Square snapped up the accolade for its warm welcome and flowing real ales under the tenure of late landlady Bridget Binnie Walsh.

Up until 1995 the pub had been known as The Welsh Harp, but when Irish Binnie took over, that was the first thing to change. The stained-glass harps on the windows remained though, with pretty hanging baskets also marking the entrance. Inside, it's standing room only, with a shelf to park your pint running parallel with the bar. Glorious oil paintings of figures in Victorian garb add a bit of pub pomp, contrasting with a modern splash of beer pump clips in a multicoloured collage above the bar. This reflects Binnie's other alteration: the canny landlady added a further six beer pumps. If regulars had requests, she browsed her contact book and sought out the suds, laying on a rotating line-up of challenging UK brews (also selling from a couple of lager taps and flagons of cider).

Ale heads aren't the only sorts you'll find here, as the Harp stays true to its musical name by serving many an artist from the nearby Coliseum (home to English National Opera) and the Royal Opera House around the corner. If you're up for some detective work, you may even find them down the pub's back alley, warming up or sharing some post-show analysis.

Although Walsh managed the harmonious pub for years, it wasn't until 2009 that she took over the freehold and started winning those prizes. She sold the Harp to Fuller's Brewery for a cool £7 million before she passed away in 2015. They obviously saw the value in this beauty of a pub, promising to uphold the cherished Harp traditions.

Address 47 Chandos Place, WC2N 4HS, +44 (0)20 7836 0291, www.harpcoventgarden.com | **Getting there** Charing Cross (Bakerloo, Northern Lines) | **Hours** Mon–Thu 10.30am–11.30pm, Fri & Sat 10.30am–midnight, Sun noon–10.30pm | **Tip** The Harp's sausage sandwiches used to be a big draw, but with a branch of world-class tapas restaurant Barrafina on the doorstep, why not stop by there for chorizo instead?

55 __ The Hunter S

Fear and loathing in north London

In modern-day London, it's hard to live life as far off the edge as Hunter S. Thompson. Clubs are closing, rents are rising and that kind of frenzied drug culture is underground, if anywhere. You won't find his style of debauchery at The Hunter S on Southgate Road either, despite the pub taking the gonzo journalist's name and with it the expectation for hard and fast drinking (and a lot more still).

Luckily, it's pretty mind-bending in here. First off, there are the stuffed animals – The Hunter S practically declared all other taxidermy-decked pubs pathetic when it opened back in 2012 with dozens of stuffed animals on the walls or perched on the bar. You'll think you've been spiked with mescaline when you clock most of a bear splayed and crawling down one wall. The rest is a mash-up of Victorian features with brand-new trappings. There's been a pub on this site for 200 years and while the old-school Perseverance was a no-frills joint with a pool room and curry nights, the team renovating The Hunter S found some striking original features hidden away, including an old-school bar. They matched that with a new engraved-copper ceiling and a vintage crystal chandelier making for one of London's more striking pub settings, especially when combined with a soundtrack of low and slow jazz.

The one place you're guaranteed to get your kicks is in the toilets. The gents invites visitors to take aim at giant lip-shaped urinals or have a peek at pics of naked women – and the genitalia are just as on show in the ladies' lav. If you're feeling prudish, stick with the bar where a solid range of spirits glistens handsomely. The Hunter S knows its booze, with owners also operating Victoria Park pub The Hemingway (what is it about suicidal American authors?) and stylish and award-winning cocktail bar Satan's Whiskers in Bethnal Green (ch. 88), where the taxidermy is a little more refined. Get stuck in. It's what Hunter S. Thompson would have wanted.

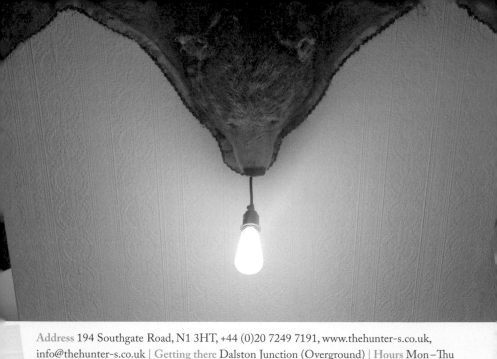

Address 194 Southgate Road, N1 3HT, +44 (0)20 7249 7191, www.thehunter-s.co.uk, info@thehunter-s.co.uk | Getting there Dalston Junction (Overground) | Hours Mon–Thu 4pm–midnight, Fri & Sat noon–1.30am, Sun noon–midnight | Tip More taxidermy weirdness can be found within easy reach at quirky Essex Road shop Get Stuffed.

56_ The Italian Job
Birra artiginale (or 'craft beer' to you)

Prosecco sales are booming in the UK, with Brits drinking the Italian grape stock dry. But in well-heeled Chiswick, they can afford Champagne, darling. That's why The Italian Job isn't popping corks and is instead serving up *birra artiginale*, Italian craft beer, on the site of a former wine bar where that Prosecco would have been a more familiar sight. But Pickwick's Wine Bar was sold up in 2015 to a group of Italians who presumably put in an offer the owner couldn't refuse.

The bar catches the eye with paintwork as blue as that eponymous movie's cliff-hanger bus, and a terrace conforming to the Italian desire to do things al fresco. Inside is a hip-for-the-area look of exposed bricks and equally exposed light bulbs. Attention is drawn to a tiled bar with six leather stools and twelve elegant beer pumps in operation. Acting as the UK's first Italian craft beer bar, it's backed by Birrificio del Ducato, one of Italy's most lauded small breweries located in Parma. The brewery was only founded in 2007 but reflects the boom in a country whose history isn't quite as heavily entwined with the humble hop. Del Ducato beers are always available on draught, along with interesting drinks from the rest of Italia. Forget the Peroni and try beers laced with local flowers, nuts and roots to create characteristic flavour. Pair half pints with Italian street food – from *torta fritta* to *arancini* – as well as imported burrata and Parma ham. Main dishes help with high-percentage beers, including popular burgers and a steak option to suit the affluent customer base. Imported beers aren't cheap, but that doesn't seem to bother folk out west.

The Chiswick formula has rolled out across London, with an Italian takeover in Mercato Metropolitano market in Elephant & Castle, a follow-up bar in Notting Hill after significant crowdfunding and a further Hackney outpost. Hang on lads, I've got a great idea.

Address 13 Devonshire Road, W4 2EU, +44 (0)20 8994 2852, www.theitalianjobpub.co.uk, info@theitalianjobpub.co.uk | Getting there Turnham Green (Circle, District, Piccadilly Lines) | Hours Mon & Tue 5–11.30pm, Wed 4–11.30pm, Thu noon–11.30pm, Fri & Sat noon–midnight, Sun 11am–11.30pm | Tip La Trompette is doing Michelin-star European eats two doors down.

57 The Ivy House

London's first co-operative

Walk into this pub on a quiet residential street in Nunhead and be taken aback as its nondescript exterior reveals a stunning Grade II-listed interior and glistening red-and-gold stage. The Ivy House first opened as the Newlands Tavern and was subsequently known as the Stuart Arms, with its musical heyday during the pub rock movement of the '70s. Once it gained its glorious music-hall stage the likes of Ian Dury, Elvis Costello and Dr Feelgood came for gigs, posters for which can be found on the walls.

But it's today's sense of community that's most impressive. On a regular Monday evening you might find a local knitting group sitting around a table sharing pointers and half pints while in a side room a chess club battles under the twinkling fairy lights. Or seek out a pub quiz, live jazz or daytime mother and baby classes. It's no wonder the locals came together almost ten years ago to save the pub in a way London had never seen before.

Upon hearing the news that The Ivy House had been put on the market in 2012, many neighbours flocked to the pub to hear more of its fate. A collective formed that day led (as if by fortune) by a solicitor, a chartered surveyor and a town planner. In the nick of time the pub was granted its status as one of the first assets of community value in the UK just months after The Localism Act had been introduced. The 'Save the Ivy House' group were given six months to raise the funds to take over the freehold through the Right to Bid scheme, and by March 2013 the group had enough to purchase the pub. They then offered shares to locals to help provide working capital to spruce the pub back up into shape.

The Ivy House now has 371 shareholders, making it the first co-operative pub in London. And it's doubtful you'll find a more cared-for place in the capital where, whatever time of day, you can practically feel the pulse of the community.

Address 40 Stuart Road, SE15 3BE, +44 (0)20 7277 8233, www.ivyhousenunhead.com, orders@ivyhousenunhead.com | Getting there Nunhead (National Rail) | Hours Mon–Thu noon–11pm, Fri & Sat noon–midnight, Sun noon–10.30pm | Tip If you're after more history in the area, neighbouring Nunhead Cemetery is one of London's Magnificent Seven cemeteries on the outskirts of the city.

58__ The Jellied Eel

Swap pie and mash for cocktails and croquetas

Pie and mash: an iconic pairing as symbolic of London's fading East End as the pearly kings and queens. Cocktails and croquetas? Not so much. But sample them at Walthamstow's Jellied Eel, and you'll be feeling all misty eyed for simpler times and Cockney rhymes. It all started in the autumn of 2018, when local east Londoner Paul Jellis, a theatre and events manager, decided to launch a pop-up bar inside L Manze pie-and-mash shop on the high street. It helped bring a piece of the city's history to the forefront of punters' minds, since that pie shop is one of only 20 eateries of its kind still standing in London from what was once a thriving empire. The recurring pop-up was popular enough with locals that it became permanent in September 2019, and it now takes over Manze's every Friday and Saturday night.

Each weekend, rickety booths fill up with parties of guests who don't mind compromising on comfort for the sake of a singular session. The lights get a filter, throwing a seedy red tone onto white tiled walls (look up to take in gorgeous art deco reliefs that run round the perimeter of the room), and the counter where hot grub is usually dispensed becomes a functioning bar. Pisco sours have become the cult cocktail at the Jellied Eel, with piquant ancho reyes liqueur added to make it a Pisco Inferno. Other cocktails are available, but this one goes down especially well with the Spanish snacks that come out hot from the kitchen. The béchamel balls beat a jellied eel any day and can be enjoyed in abundance, since seven different varieties of the deep-fried delicacy are available.

In the summer, a good's yard at the back gets turned into a bench-filled garden, an ideal setting in which to enjoy tapas and tipples. But really you should visit for a cosy, atmospheric drink indoors. The bar is bringing a new generation of fans into Manze's for a completely different kind of liquor.

Address Manze's Pie & Mash, 76 High Street, E17 7LD, www.thejelliedeel.com, bookings@thejelliedeel.com | **Getting there** Walthamstow Central (Victoria Line) | **Hours** Fri & Sat 7pm – midnight | **Tip** Even more art deco exists in the area – a stunning former cinema and theatre that is being transformed into a 1,000 capacity comedy venue, set to open in 2022.

59 Jerusalem Tavern
Confusing but nonetheless charming history

Two twee benches sit outside the old-fashioned bookshop façade of Jerusalem Tavern, but readers rarely populate them. A little arched passageway runs down the side of this Clerkenwell building and the overall effect is positively picturesque, like something you'd expect to see on a postcard. And on the moss green shopfront written in gold, a sign reads, 'anno 1720'. As such, this pub of sorts is full of surprises.

For starters, the interior isn't from 1720 at all. Yet you'd be forgiven for believing the company line. The building has indeed been around for centuries, but it was given its most recent spruce-up in 1992 when a café tried to recreate the look of an 18th-century coffee house in keeping with the building's origins. When the Jerusalem Tavern took over in 1996 the team chose to keep the well-worn look. So you'll find a dinky room segmented into dinkier nooks by wood and glass panelling, bare plaster walls livened up by blue-on-white Dutch tiles, a wood-burning fireplace and scuffed-up floorboards. It's the kind of place suited for our littler ancestors, and squeezing into a spare seat is all part of the experience.

The second surprise is that the shelves are stocked with beer as opposed to books. But the heavy, yeasty smell in the air gives up the game that this is an ale-ficionados' paradise. It's the only pub owned by St Peter's Brewery of Suffolk and you can spy small barrels of organic and interesting ale tapped behind the bar and served at room temperature. You can gaze down on charming country-pub-style service from a small mezzanine slightly raised above the bar that just about fits a table and chairs for two. Many local designers, architects and even history buffs visit to marvel at the tradition of it all without knowing that its name comes from an inn that had been in the area on and off since the 14th century. It's a tangled old history, but one well worth drinking to.

Address 55 Briton Street, EC1M 5UQ, +44 (0)20 7490 4281, www.stpetersbrewery.co.uk, thejerusalemtavern@gmail.com | Getting there Farringdon (Circle, Hammermsith & City, Metropolitan Lines, National Rail) | Hours Mon – Fri 11am – 11pm | Tip History also echoes through the building at popular Smithfield restaurant St John, which through the years has been *Marxism Today's* HQ, a smokehouse and a Chinese beer store but is now better known for first-rate British grub.

60__Kanpai London Sake Taproom

Sake to me

While many people claim their travels have been 'life-changing', not all of them have gone to the extremes that Lucy and Tom Wilson have to continue that post-holiday high. The married pair fell in love with sake, the Japanese rice wine, when they travelled around the country visiting craft sake breweries along the way. Upon their return, they began experimenting with home brewing (Tom had already dabbled with beer making in the past), launching the UK's first craft sake in 2017 and naming their operation Kanpai (Japanese for 'cheers'). They scaled up to larger brewing premises in Peckham's Copeland Park in 2018, where they've been producing three sakes core to their range ever since, as well as seasonal specials.

It's in this industrial HQ that the couple also operate a buzzy taproom on Friday nights and on Saturdays throughout the day. It sits above all the paraphernalia of sake making – from koshiki steaming vats to koji stock – and under the warehouse's corrugated canopy. It's divided in two; a more studious tasting room and event space on one side and a small bar with a large shared table on the other. Back on ground level, there are benches scattered just beyond the brewery's door, filled with drinkers in the summer who have Kanpai's bold Japan-inspired graffiti for a backdrop. Down here, there's even a fully functioning, jet-powered Japanese toilet.

From the bar, you can sample the core range of Kanpai sake in a flight of three, which the Wilsons will likely talk you through – they're often found working in their place of passion. You can also delve into other Japanese rice wines, plus sake served in fruity cocktails. Or enjoy the drink paired with a bowl of ramen. It's easy to go all-out with your immersion into sake in south east London, and even easier to see what attracted Lucy and Tom to the trend.

Address Unit 2A-2, 133 Copeland Road, SE15 3SN, www.kanpai.london, hello@kanpailondon.co.uk | Getting there Peckham Rye (Overground Lines, National Rail) | Hours Fri 5–10.30pm, Sat noon–10.30pm | Tip It's all about craft brewing in Peckham right now. Check out beers by Brick brewery or head to the tasting room of Gosnells mead brewery.

61__Little Nan's Bar
Party like a pensioner

Princess Di and Pat Butcher have somehow become synonymous with good times at Deptford's Little Nan's Bar. The unlikely homage to these British legends – one the queen of hearts, the other the queen of tarts – is all part and parcel of an off-the-wall idea of theming a bar on an old dear's living room. The concept comes from local lad Tristan Scutt, and his bar is in loving memory of his 'little nan' Josephine. As such, see a jumble of kitsch cat cushions, the royal family in photo frames and a wall of proud grandparent trophies among clashing armchairs, poufs and doily-topped tables.

But there's more to this bar than a corny theme and more to warm the cockles than a lad who loves his grandmother; it's a homecoming story, too. Little Nan's Bar started out in 2013 as a pop-up on Deptford High Street, a ramshackle room rented from a neighbouring club. The unique theme was an instant success, but the council shut down the operation in 2014 due to licensing issues with the club's landlord. And so Little Nan's roamed around east London hosting spin-offs of the original pop-up until three years later, when developments began on Deptford's railway arches and the opportunity arose for Little Nan's to return triumphantly to the 'hood.

The bar is ever evolving to keep up with the pace of Scutt's imagination. Since launch they've introduced bottomless brunch, karaoke nights and a golden bust of 'Queen Pat' for decoration. And the bar now has 'Grandad's Shed' next door, available for private hire. Afternoon tea is served from commemorative crockery, teapots spiked with fizzy cocktails that take their names from other *EastEnders* characters (anyone for a Lord Beppe Di Marco?). Daytime crochet classes turn to Abba and Spice Girls sing-alongs. And in honour of that theme, Scutt makes this a family affair with his cousin baking scones, his mum making jam and his former Goldsmiths uni pals chipping in with that retro design. Nan would be proud.

Address Arches 13–14, Deptford Market Yard, SE8 4BX, www.littlenans.co.uk, littlenansbar@gmail.com | **Getting there** Deptford Rail (National Rail) | **Hours** Mon–Fri 3–11pm, Sat noon–11pm, Sun noon–10pm | **Tip** For more cheesiness in Deptford, head over to Taproom SE8, where the pizzas complement the beers very nicely.

62__Lyaness

Glam hotel setting, game-changing cocktails

Forget everything you thought you knew about hotel bars; Lyaness at the South Bank's Sea Containers has changed the game. It combines a trad view across the Thames and over to St Paul's with a contemporary interior. Pastel blue walls and ultramarine crushed-velvet seats clash unapologetically with a marsh-green bar and brash gold railings. It's as if Wes Anderson's colour palette has been let loose on a hotel bar. Meanwhile, the drinks are less Wes more Willy Wonka. Cocktails served by award-winning staff are made from a set of seven wacky core 'ingredients', like 'infinite banana', 'purple pineapple' and 'peach emoji'. Yet none of this will surprise anyone who's come across the name Ryan Chetiyawardana before.

Ryan C., aka Mr Lyan, is one of the best-known mixologists in London (or indeed, on the planet), and while you won't necessarily see him making drinks, you'll get a taste of his creativity from one sip at his London bar. Lyaness can be seen as sort of an evolution, launching on the exact same site as 'World's Best Bar' Dandelyan in 2018, also in the Mr Lyan family. And before that was White Lyan in Hoxton, a hip, low-key east London bar launching towards the start of the decade within a former pub and quietly breaking the mixed-drink mould.

As with Dandelyan and White Lyan before it, Lyaness shares the same values of sustainability and creativity. The virtually zero-waste bar changes menus with the seasons and themes its drinks around its cause and around out-there cocktail making processes. That's how you'll find yourself sipping on these madcap ingredients that together taste like the best drink of your life. A story sits behind each sip with every member of the team having helped shape the imaginative list and narrating as they deliver drinks. If you're spoilt for choice, a chart on the menu suggests a time of day for each tipple. But in truth, you'll never go wrong at Lyaness.

Address Sea Containers London, 20 Upper Ground, SE1 9PD, +44 (0)20 3747 1063, www.lyaness.com, reservations@seacontainerslondon.com | Getting there Blackfriars (Circle, District Lines, National Rail) | Hours Mon–Wed 4pm–1am, Thu–Sat noon–2am, Sun noon–12.30am | Tip For more of those St Paul's views, venture to the Tate Modern's viewing platform.

63 Mahogany Bar

Polished up quite nicely

The Mahogany Bar is the oldest part of the oldest surviving music hall in London. And even though its current look dates back only to 2009, the faded glamour of its wooden ceiling and handsomely peeling walls honours both that history and how it stood derelict and unloved for half a century.

Originally an ale house serving sea captains and merchants in the 1690s, the bar carried many names – the Prince of Denmark, the Albion Saloon – until its eponymous bar, an out-of-the-ordinary mahogany fitting detailed with intricate patterns, was installed in 1828. It was there to greet visitors during the building's heyday from the 1850s to the 1880s, after John Wilton bought the place and added its famed music hall. The stars rolled in to Wilton's for glitzy plays and cabaret shows (Champagne Charlie singer George Leybourne included) in the jaw-dropping setting of grand chandeliers, mirrors and curtains. But after a serious fire in 1877, Wilton's never returned to its glory. Having had its moment in the spotlight, the venue closed in 1881. Isn't showbiz fickle?

Soon after, the East London Methodist Mission bought the building, spending 70 years here campaigning against social injustices, using the Mahogany Bar as a soup kitchen. Its last guise was as a rag warehouse when the council proposed to knock down the building in the '60s. Even though campaigners saved it, Wilton's remained unoccupied and derelict, unfit for public use, until it gradually reopened at the turn of the century and after a whole lot of investment. By 1997 an audience was finally invited back into the theatre, and slowly, other parts of the building became safe again.

The bar now hosts live music, serves theatre-goers pizza and lager in the interval and welcomes those visiting for just a glimpse of its magic. Best of all, that precious mahogany bar has truly stood the test of time.

Address Wilton's Music Hall, 1 Graces Alley, E1 8JB, +44 (0)20 7702 2789, www.wiltons.org.uk, bar@wiltons.org.uk | **Getting there** Tower Hill (Circle, District Lines) | **Hours** Mon – Sat 5pm – 11pm | **Tip** To witness a Whitechapel legend almost as sprawling, head to Tayyabs, a long-standing Punjabi restaurant.

64_Mayflower

Creaking piece of pub history on the River Thames

The Mayflower deserves a prize for being one of London's oldest pubs that actually feels as ancient as it is, and all in a charming way. Even walking the cobbled backstreets of Rotherhithe to get to this hidden-away Thames-side hostelry has a quaint yesteryear feel to it. But once inside, prepare to have your breath taken away – or your head knocked off – by the low-beamed, creaking and downright beautiful appearance of this restored, 400-odd-year-old inn.

Come at nighttime to appreciate the Mayflower in all its glory. Lit by flickering candlelight from lamps and chandeliers hanging overhead, you could truly get lost in one of the pub's atmospheric nooks or in its snug room. An upstairs dining room offers a bit more light on matters, especially when lattice windows are flung open to reveal quite the view across the Thames, but we recommend taking to the pub's jetty deck downstairs to really soak up the waterside scene. It's right by this spot that the *Mayflower* ship supposedly set sail to Plymouth in 1620, before the Pilgrims embarked on their maiden voyage to the Americas.

That may explain why the deck flies the Star-Spangled Banner, and how The Mayflower came to be the only place licensed to sell American postage stamps in the UK. So vie for a seat on this historic deck for the real deal, especially with the tide rolling in and lapping beneath your feet. Just as authentic an experience is getting cosy by the fire in winter with a plate of British cheeses and a pint of one of the four regularly changing and well-kept guest ales.

Having said all of that, you'll still find the odd trappings of a modern pub, like blankets and patio heaters to stave off the London chill on deck or a lively weeknight quiz back indoors. And look out for Eliza, a pub cat almost too young-looking for her surroundings, and Ringo, a hound who often appears on the pub's social media accounts and who is a bit more suitably disheveled.

Address 117 Rotherhithe Street, SE16 4NF, +44 (0)20 7237 4088, www.mayflowerpub.co.uk, info@mayflowerpub.co.uk | Getting there Rotherhithe (Overground) | Hours Mon–Sat 11am–11pm, Sun noon–10.30pm | Tip The Mayflower is on the Thames Path, a walking route past many of London's historic river pubs. Don't miss the Prospect of Whitby in Wapping for similar beauty.

65 __ Milk & Honey

London's original speakeasy

Finding the entrance is the first challenge. There's not a lot giving away this cocktail lounge spread across four floors of a Soho townhouse. Press the buzzer then enter with trepidation to a reception desk with a velvet drape blocking your view. Give your name – there's no way you're getting in without a reservation – and be led to a stunning setting so dark you'll have to strain to see. Candlelight bounces from dimpled wall tiles and low gold ceilings, staff dress in shirts and braces, soft jazz murmurs and booths provide more secrecy. There's no doubting this is Prohibition, baby.

Milk & Honey was the first lounge to bring a speakeasy theme to London, in 2002. It's a member's bar open to Average Joe until 11pm. Punters can enjoy the ground floor or the black-as-night basement, while members have a first-floor space named 'the red room' like something from *Fifty Shades of Grey*. The idea came at the turn of the millennium when bar entrepreneur Jonathan Downey took a trip to New York. Downey already had a string of scene-defining bars in London. But it was a visit to a new and secretive bar called Milk & Honey in Manhattan's Lower East Side that inspired him to team up with its creator, the late Sasha Petraske, to bring the concept to London.

This speakeasy sister defined a London trend. It came with its own set of house rules ('gentlemen will not introduce themselves to ladies' etc.), which seem slightly dated now. But the cocktail menu originally devised by American drinks-whizz Dale Degroff has stood the test of time, with this bar the training ground for some of London's finest bartenders. Downey has since moved from cocktail bars to street-food markets, and Milk & Honey has a miniature outpost at one of his Street Feast sites. But for authenticity, head to Soho. The imitators might come and go, but Milk & Honey is peak Prohibition.

Address 61 Poland Street, W1F 7NU, +44 (0)20 7065 6800, www.mlkhny.com, bookings@rshmr.com | **Getting there** Oxford Circus (Bakerloo, Central, Victoria Lines) | **Hours** Mon–Sat 6pm–3am (6–11pm non-members, by reservation only) | **Tip** Find street food in a restaurant setting just moments from Milk & Honey. Bao does Taiwanese street eats and always has a queue out the door.

66 ___ Milroy's of Soho

A wee dram behind the bookcase

It's the sweet oaky smell that gives the first clue that Milroy's of Soho has been around a while. Opening in 1964, it's London's oldest whisky shop, with founders and brothers Jack and Wallace Milroy monumental to the UK's single malt revolution. The brothers would drive a van to Scotland bringing back single malts at a time when blends were all people could get their hands on. Soon their wine shop moved from grape to grain and became known for the largest whisky collection in the capital, with the pair going on to be global names in the drinks industry.

The Milroy brothers sold the shop in the '90s and the place lost touch with its whisky-loving roots, but in 2013, Milroy's was taken over by Martyn 'Simo' Simpson, a local restaurateur keen to save a slice of Soho history. With his arrival came a reinstated 12-seater first-floor bar where fanatics can sample over 250 drams. He also brought with him Chester, a Jack Russell he bought from a homeless man on Soho's streets, who now follows him faithfully round the shop. And Simo created The Vault of Soho, a dimly lit, bare-brick hangout in the basement with a focus on premium cocktails made by industry-best bartenders. Simo describes it as 'Soho's worst-kept secret' since it's a firm late-night favourite with local restaurant staff. There's no signage giving away its presence and – like all good things – it's hidden behind a bookcase at the back of the shop.

And as for the shop, go at any time of day and you'll find a stream of customers from around the world and of all ages. Deliveries were once made from here to 10 Downing Street, but modern day clients include Lindsay Lohan and Dermot O'Leary, who even has his own whisky locker to stash a bottle for the next visit. He's sure to embrace the Milroy's expansion, with a spin-off tasting room recently launching across town in Spitalfields.

Address 3 Greek Street, W1D 4NX, www.thevaultsoho.co.uk,
reservations@thevaultsoho.co.uk | **Getting there** Tottenham Court Road (Central,
Northern Lines) | **Hours** Mon 10am–7pm, Tue–Sat 10am–12am | **Tip** Delve deeper
into quality spirits at Old Compton Street's Gerry's a nearby off-licence, selling
interesting bottles from all over the world since 1984.

67 Mr Fogg's Gin Parlour

London's Gin Craze, part 2

'Mother's ruin': a name that symbolises the bad reputation gin had gained during its production boom in 18th-century London. As the so-called 'Gin Craze' reached its height, poorer-quality versions of the spirit were lapped up by the lower classes with a scale of public drunkenness that worried Parliament. The fear was best depicted in Hogarth's semi-propagandistic print, *Gin Lane*, a scene of destruction, death and depravity set in Bloomsbury that contrasted with the harmony of *Beer Lane*. Subsequently, the Gin Act of 1751 clamped down on small-batch distillers and the craze began to wane.

The tide only turned in 2009, when Hammersmith distiller Sipsmith was granted the licence to produce gin on a small scale. Distilleries have since cropped up all over the capital starting a slightly more sophisticated craft gin craze. Proof comes just around the corner from Hogarth's mythical Gin Lane at Mr Fogg's Gin Parlour, a quirky upstairs den in Covent Garden and a very different scene fuelled by the same spirit. The bar opened in 2015 claiming London's largest collection of gins on its 'Encyclopaedia Gintonica' menu, with over 300 varieties in stock. The drinks list divvies up a library of spirits by style so ginthusiasts can pick from 'fruity', 'vintage' and 'Old Tom' flavours and pair them with a full fleet of botanicals and tonics.

Expensive-looking chaises longues, frilly lampshades, damask curtains and chintz wallpaper make up the Victorian-style salon, with opera music piped through. It's slightly gimmicky – roleplaying staff keep up the convoluted act that this parlour belongs to Phileas Fogg's Great Aunt Gertrude – but there's boozy afternoon tea and 'gin safari' master classes for sophisticated entertainment. Down below is Mr Fogg's Tavern, a Dickensian pub serving pies and beers to the masses. It's almost as if Hogarth's famous works have been flipped.

Address 1 New Row, WC2N 4EA, +44 (0)20 7590 3605, www.mr-foggs.com/
gin-parlour, ginparlour@mr-foggs.com | Getting there Covent Garden (Piccadilly Line) |
Hours Mon–Fri 5pm–midnight, Sat 3pm–midnight, Sun 5pm–10.30pm | Tip Head over
to Holborn Dining Room, a nearby restaurant with a sweeping bar that has a gin collection
to rival Mr Fogg's spirit stash.

68___The Nags Head

Knickknacks and no phones

Rule-breakers should try their best to behave at this lovable inn, as the rules applied by the free house's landlord Kevin Moran only enhance the experience: 1) Hang your coat on one of the pub's many hooks and 2) No mobile phones. Tatty posters using '90s clipart advertise these stipulations on the walls and at the entrance, so there's no excuse. And you can bet you'll get a rap on the knuckles if caught by Moran and his wife, who've been laying down the law for over 25 years. Still, it takes some restraint not to pull out your smartphone and get snapping the first time you visit this grotto of memorabilia – it's like Father Christmas got a penchant for World War II and the era's pin-up girls and rockabilly singers. You'll find faces cut out of magazines and plastered to the ceiling, while the bar displays that wartime tat – from medals to hats and pewter mugs.

An old stove fire from the 1820s adds to the time-warp effect with cushioned fireplace fenders for maximum cosiness. The architectural layout is a hangover from years gone by, with the bar straddling two levels and thus only reaching waist height in the ground-floor snug where staff pour Adnams from Chelsea Pottery handpumps. This split-level service was likely to accommodate stable hands and footmen in the 19th century, since the Nags Head occupies a cobbled backroad mews.

If you find yourself missing entertainment from your phone, there are plenty of characters – from suited and booted patrons who've been popping in for years to clever shoppers swapping Knightsbridge for the low hum of folk music. For something more visual, there are cartoon strips and titillating letters to Moran on the walls. Speaking of titillation, ask staff for old denomination coins to operate a 'What the Butler Saw' machine, a wooden peep-show box on the wall. Just because the Nags Head has rules doesn't mean you can't have fun.

Address 53 Kinnerton Street, SW1X 8ED, +44 (0)20 7235 1135 | Getting there Hyde Park
Corner (Piccadilly Line) | Hours Daily 11am–11pm | Tip It seems all rules have gone out
the window at Knightbridge's swanky restaurant Sumosan Twiga, which blends Japanese
and Italian cuisines.

69__Noble Rot

Wine with attitude

When a bar's run by the editors of a wine rag, you can guess you're in safe hands. When it's run by the team behind an avant-garde magazine dedicated to wine, food and culture with the likes of writers Caitlin Moran and John Niven, Mike D from the Beastie Boys and James Murphy from LCD Soundsytem among contributors, even better. Introducing Noble Rot, London's edgiest wine bar on the most unlikely old-school street, in among a tailor, a funeral director and a feminist bookshop.

The pair behind Noble Rot – the magazine and the bar – are Mark Andrew and Daniel Keeling, who met in the tasting room of Roberson Wine merchants where Andrew was head buyer. Keeling worked nearby as MD for Island Records. Their passion for talking about wine as you would about film, music and pop culture spilled over and *Noble Rot* magazine was born in 2013. The bold-looking publication was rebellious within the wine world but chimed with many, the second issue receiving £11,600 of Kickstarter funding. They clearly had a captive audience, so a wine bar was a welcome step.

Taking their cue from Paris wine bar-bistros, they enlisted chef Stephen Harris from famed seaside gastropub The Sportsman, along with his unique take on oysters and slip sole. His menu brings out the best in the wine, but it's the bar at the front that deserves attention, a room that has kept the wonky wooden floor, fireplace and moss-green walls from the building's former life as ageing wine bar Vats. They've added defiant splashes of colour from framed *Noble Rot* mag covers. Perches behind the bar hold harder-to-find bottles from the likes of Tenerife as well as more common drops from the Jura. They're sold by the glass at competitive prices, the more expensive bottles given a smaller profit margin so punters can try them. The cheapest on the menu is just £2 (and delicious!). Wine times are a-changing.

Address 51 Lamb's Conduit Street, WC1N 3NB, +44 (0)20 7242 8963, www.noblerot.co.uk,
reservations@noblerot.co.uk | **Getting there** Russell Square (Piccadilly Line) | **Hours**
Mon–Sat noon–11pm | **Tip** Aesop over the road is doing similarly edgy things in the
world of soap and fragrance.

70_Opium
Smokin' cocktails

Get your fix of daring drinking in Chinatown at this lavish imagining of an illegal opium den. Three floors of madly embellished Chinese rooms await you behind an unmarked jade-green door on Gerrard Street.

Opium opened in 2012 in a central townhouse, whose illicit past functions include that of a gambling den. Whether it was used for chasing the dragon is unlikely – those venues seem to have been more widespread in literature, although it's thought a handful of opium dens existed further east in Victorian times. Opium is not entirely dissimilar, though; this operation is all about cocktails that twist elements of East and West in mind-bending ways across its many lairs, and guests tend to be the curious sort.

There's The Apothecary Bar on the first floor with little red drawers all in a row acting as the back-bar, libations poured into medicinal bottles carrying Chinese characters on the labels. For more ordered imbibing, there's a tearoom pouring specialist blends from Postcard Teas into beautiful blue-and-white porcelain. A dim sum dining room was added to the venue not long after launch and serves Chinese snacks until 3am, whipped up by an undisclosed Chinatown restaurant. And a speakeasy joined the set, named Peony (after the delicate flower whose root is used in traditional Chinese medicine). If you're carrying out a late-night tryst, after all, where better than a speakeasy within a secret bar?

But the real wizardry is reserved for the bartender's table in the attic. When the bar launched, cocktail expert Dre Masso was on the team concocting tipples with Asian ingredients, dry ice and an overactive imagination (in a good way!). His star 'Opium' drinks are a series of self-smoking cocktails served in mini black cauldrons. If that's not gimmick enough, venture to the toilets and get barked at in Cantonese over the speakers. One of many ways to get a buzz at Opium.

Address 15–16 Gerrard Street, W1D 6JE, www.opiumchinatown.com, reservations@opiumchinatown.com | Getting there Leicester Square (Northern, Piccadilly Lines) | Hours Mon & Tue 5pm–1am, Wed 5pm–2am, Thu–Sat 5pm–3am, Sun 5pm–midnight | Tip While Chinatown is full of restaurants for a quick bite, treat yourself to Michelin-star Chinese grub at Yauatcha in Soho, away from the tourist trail.

71___Original Sin

Can you Adam and Eve it?

Happiness Forgets is one of the capital's pioneering cocktail bars, taking its cool cue from New York's neighbourhood bar scene when it launched in 2010. The idea was to bring exemplary cocktails to a down-to-earth, hard-to-find basement on the edge of the centre of town, and it still does that so convincingly, consistently named one of the best bars in the world. But for more intrepid drinking, venture away from Hoxton Square to Ali Burgess' follow-up bar in Stoke Newington. Original Sin is the naughty little sister, the hip young thing.

An unmarked doorway along the High Street leads you into the darkness and down to the fun. It's a narrow but surprisingly large space, with room for booth seats lined up in a row in the style of an old rail carriage. You'll be gagging to get on board when you read from a list of innovative and invigorating cocktails, which are served at knockdown prices during a daily happy hour. They're all pretty potent in the best possible way, and you shouldn't expect your usual gin fizz or whisky sour, with the bar choosing more unusual spirits to pep things up. Instead, find cocktails made from armagnac, amaro, aquavit and apple brandy mixed with white cacao, tomato cordial, pomegranate molasses and the like.

Original Sin's pièce de résistance is an American pool table at the opposite end of the room to the bar, where you won't need a stack of quarters to get in on the action. It's free to use, further cementing the bar's community spirit. The fact that it's barely lit by little pineapple-shaped lights on the walls only enhances the opportunities for a flirtatious game with Stokey strangers. Best of all is the team of staff, heavily tattooed and dressed in New York-style brown aprons. Yeah, they're a cool crew, but they're also friends you're yet to make. Even if everyone is born with a sinful streak, these lot are good as gold to customers.

Address 129 Stoke Newington High Street, N16 0PH, www.originalsin.bar, reservations@originalsin.bar | Getting there London Bridge (Jubilee, Northern Lines) | Hours Mon 6–11pm, Tue & Wed 6pm–midnight, Thu–Sat 6pm–1.30am, Sun 6–11pm | Tip Just over the road is another great cocktail spot. Yet the Mint Gun Club is the polar opposite to Original Sin, a light, bright space for daytime imbibing.

72 Palm Tree
East End relic

Out towards Mile End in a derelict stretch by Regent's Canal before it hits the Limehouse Basin you'll find the most unlikely location for an authentic East End singalong round the old 'Joanna'. That's 'piano', for those less acquainted with Cockney rhyming slang, and you should probably brush up on yours before a trip to The Palm Tree. This pub from the 1930s was originally a part of the Truman Brewery portfolio and looks fairly unremarkable to passersby, an isolated building with no neighbours to mention and few distinguishing external features. It certainly doesn't scream 'knees up Mother Brown'. But as the sole survivor of the Blitz along this road and with Grade II-listed status since 2015, it's clear this old pub shouldn't be underestimated.

You'll only have this confirmed upon entering the Palm Tree, which is divided into two dimly lit, red-hued rooms, a view through to either offered from a vantage point at the horseshoe bar. Said bar is framed by signed black-and-white portraits of jockeys and West End stars from a bygone era. They're not the only relics though, with red velvet curtains unlike any you'll find in IKEA, gold chintz wallpaper and an antique cash register. Come flashing your plastic at this cash-only bar and it's likely you'll get laughed out the building by staff.

What you'll spend your money on is of minor concern though, as it's all about an atmosphere that's hard to find anywhere else in London. Jolly good show, as ales aren't always kept in the best condition; perhaps stick with the bottled continental lagers, which you can take outside to join the crowds by the canal on sunnier days. Or venture inside to the bar on the right to see all shades of local life. It's like an *EastEnders* scene in here, especially on Saturday nights as a jazz band trio occupies the pub for a riotous evening of trad live music and Cockney ditties.

Address 127 Grove Road, E3 5RP, +44 (0)20 8980 2918 | Getting there Mile End (Central, District, Hammersmith & City Lines) | Hours Mon–Sat 12.30–11pm, Sun 12.30–10.30pm | Tip Complete the classic East End experience with fish and chips at Grove Road's Britannia Fish Bar.

73__ The Pelton Arms
…or is it the Nag's Head?

Just off the Thames Path and away from the tourist trail is a pub that marks itself as 'The Nag's Head'. But confusingly, this is The Pelton Arms. So why the long face? Back in 2011, the pub was used for filming *Only Fool's and Horses* spin-off show *Rock and Chips,* and the signage has stayed ever since. On the wall is a cardboard mask of Boycie's face signed by actor John Challis who played Del Boy and Rodney's pal. Apparently he's not the only star to have frequented The Pelton, since Hollywood legends Frank Sinatra, Tony Curtis and Kirk Douglas are said to have stopped by between takes for *The List of Adrian Messenger.* Away from Hollywood, the Pelton has a reputation on the music scene, having supported up-and-coming acts as well as old favourites – Deptford band Squeeze performed a warm-up gig before their UK tour on the pub's small stage back in 2012.

The Pelton's entertainment agenda is down to music-loving landlord Geoff Keen. He took over the pub in 2010 and gave the L-shaped space an indie look in a part of town where much else is homogenised. Instead of Cutty Sark portraits, expect archive photos of the working-class docklands. In lieu of prim and proper furniture find battered, second-hand armchairs. In place of calligraphy, see the Pelton's name in red neon. And although there's taxidermy, the pub's mounted stag wears a deerstalker or policeman's hat for comedy effect.

A popular weeknight pub quiz sees tables booked in advance, or try more sedate action during knitting club or over a game of bar billiards or darts. The Pelton also hosts beer festivals, bake-offs and Northern Soul nights. As such, it's a shame to learn such an entertaining pub was under fire from new neighbours for its noise levels back in 2016, which resulted in Keen putting the pub on the market. But luckily, the spell he cast on The Pelton seems to have lived on, despite the neighbours. The pub still regularly rocks.

Address 23–25 Pelton Road, SE10 9PQ, +44 (0)20 8858 0572, www.peltonarms.com |
Getting there Greenwich (DLR Line) | **Hours** Mon–Thu noon–midnight, Fri & Sat
noon–1am, Sun noon–11pm | **Tip** *Only Fools and Horses* fans should head to Acton's
Harlech Tower to observe Rodney and Del Boy's fictional Mandela House from the outside.

74_Phoenix Artist Club

One for the theatre luvvies

There's really no business like show business. Go to the Phoenix Artist Club to see this in action. The unassuming entrance is just off gritty Charing Cross Road and upstaged by the Phoenix Theatre's front doors, but don't let this downplayed start put you off. You're usually guaranteed some form of theatricality on the door from lively staff, and you'll descend a blingy set of stairs to a darkened room lit by stage spotlights and Hollywood smiles.

Those gleaming grins come from signed photos from the stars of the stage that plaster every last inch of wall right up to the ceiling. Red velvet chairs and a neon hue behind the bar add even more show-biz glitz, but you'll probably be more dedicated to people-watching. Past patrons of the Phoenix allegedly include the likes of Lady Gaga, and on any given night you'll find wrap parties for screen and stage. Spot the Darth Vader mask on the wall from a *Star Wars* bash for proof. It also hosted after-parties for gigs at the now-demolished Astoria – the Arctic Monkeys getting turned away on the door of their own event for looking too scruffy.

However, the venue may be best known for staying open much later than surrounding West End bars, with older luvvies still refer-ring to the Phoenix as 'Shuts' (because it never does). Many also flock here for weekly open-mic sing-alongs, where you may catch the stars of *The Book of Mormon* performing songs from *Wicked*, in among ambitious musical theatre kids. In full, The Phoenix is no place for the shy and retiring; even the club's late manager and bon vivant Maurice Huggett was famed for his larger-than-life persona (and his waistcoat collection). His picture now hangs proudly by the bar.

Although it's a member's bar, the venue welcomes all walks of life through its doors until 8pm. But if you really want the backstage goss, get that membership sorted pronto.

Address 1 Phoenix Street, WC2H 8BU, +44 (0)20 7836 1077, www.phoenixartistclub.com, reservations@phoenixartistclub.com | **Getting there** Tottenham Court Road (Central, Northern Lines) | **Hours** Mon–Sat 10.30am–2.30am, Sun noon–1.30am | **Tip** Disrepute in Kingly Court is another central London 'member's bar' with a similarly loose interpretation of the term and with late-night opening hours to boot.

75__Pineapple

Fruity old pub with a famous following

Turquoise-coloured corner pub the Pineapple spells sanctuary to passersby in what is already quite the desirable neighbourhood in Kentish Town; all terrace houses, peace and quiet. A pineapple illustration swings proudly above the door, marking out a quirky anomaly in traditional north London.

The Pineapple has held this prominent position since 1868, and began as a haven to new locals working on the rail lines in the area. It held Easter bonnet competitions, fancy dress parties and even meet-ups for the local pigeon-fancier club. It's fair to say the typical patron has evolved from working-class grafter to middle-class settler, but you'll still find devotees from those glory days occupying the cosy front section. These are the ones who grouped together to save the pub in 2001 after landlady Mary Gately sold up on the false promise that the pub would remain. This group inspired a number of famous punters – from Jon Snow to Ken Loach – to speak up against the pub's threatened closure, and within eight days of the story making the national press, English Heritage had granted a Grade II listing.

You'll now find a plaque on the wall honouring that tumultuous time ('The Pineapple War 2001–2002'). You'll also find period features as you push back the theatrical curtain and face the imposing, old-fashioned bar backed with mirrors and lettering offering 'wines, brandies, whiskies'. Passageways run down either side with alcoves warmed by an open fire and genial chat. There's a modern conservatory to the rear, the best place to tuck into an equally modern Thai menu. And an upstairs event space doubles as an occasional practice ground for comedians testing new material, from Josh Widdicombe to Katherine Ryan. There's even a cheese night (sans pineapple) on Tuesdays. The Pineapple stands out on the inside just as much as it does on sleepy Leverton Street.

Address 51 Leverton Street, NW5 2NX, +44 (0)20 7284 4631, www.facebook.com/
thepineapplepub | Getting there Kentish Town (Overground, National Rail) | Hours
Mon–Thu noon–11pm, Fri & Sat noon–midnight, Sun noon–10.30pm | Tip Although
it's nowhere near as cosy, the Pineapple has spawned a sister pub in Camden called the Lady
Hamilton. Visit for a more modern take on hospitality – including bao buns and craft beer.

76   The Pink Chihuahua

Secretive Day of the Dead den

All the best bars are the ones kept secret, but how many secrets are left in London these days? Well, it feels like the cat – or the miniature dog – has never been truly let out of the bag on this basement bar in Soho honouring Mexican drinking culture. The Pink Chihuahua is hidden underneath Baja California-tinged El Camión restaurant and specialises (perhaps predictably) in tequila. But the way it has done so over the years is anything but predictable thanks to its association with the late cocktail legend Dick Bradsell.

El Camión and its wicked basement bar were launched in 2009 as the second Mexican in London from Ned Conran, son of design mogul Sir Terrence Conran. He obviously knew a thing or two about the power of a big name, aiming high in approaching Bradsell – Soho's bar star who invented the Bramble and the espresso martini – to run the basement with free reign. Bradsell named the bar and created a tequila-based, pink-hued pomegranate drink to match. He was known to cross-dress on Day of the Dead and his cult of personality attracted the likes of Jarvis Cocker and Twiggy down the stairs for a drink.

Perhaps the Chihuahua is still fairly secret since it's a member's bar, but it's hardly an uptight, exclusive joint. Expect a welcome from wildly bright Mexican iconography and a clientele of equally colourful Soho hospitality staff who've clocked off for the evening and are looking to get their own kicks in the neighbourhood. There are over 300 rare tequilas and a whole host of mezcals in the stockrooms and in cabinets by the bar, and the cocktail menu lists batidas, margaritas and daiquiris. Bradsell sadly passed away in 2016, but the bar honours his legend with a page of his cocktails titled 'Fun with Dick'. It'll be fun indeed, with the Mexican fiesta raging on until 3am any given night of the week. Forget 'arriba!' – it's all about getting on down to The Pink Chihuahua.

Address 25–27 Brewer Street, W1F 0RR, +44 (0)20 7734 7711, www.elcamion.co.uk |
Getting there Piccadilly Circus (Bakerloo, Piccadilly Lines) | Hours Mon–Sat 6pm–3am |
Tip For more Mexican good times, La Bodega Negra restaurant on Old Compton Street
looks more like a sex shop on the outside. Dare to enter.

77__Punch Room
Prepare to be bowled over

Punch: the stuff of American frat houses or suburban '70s dinner parties. Yet the Punch Room may just be London's most fashionable bar. The drinks served here take a lot of beating, far from bowls spiked with... well, who knows? The fumed-oak-panelled room is tucked neatly to the rear of the flashy London Edition hotel, the bar so exclusive, visits are by appointment only. Yet despite this high standing and the look of a 19th-century gents club (fireplace included) a drink here is exceptionally down to earth, staff welcoming you with a complimentary sherry glass of the punch of the day. Whether you continue with punch is up to you – beer and wine are happily served – but to veer away from London's drink du jour in the capital's only dedicated punch bar would be remiss.

The vision comes from Italian bar manager Davide Segat, who consulted books on the art of punch-making and recipes dating as far back as the 17th century, compiling a spreadsheet of over 150 drinks. His work forms a menu named 'The Five', a succinct cocktail list presented as a novel. The word 'punch' comes from the Sanskrit for 'five', as influenced by its five traditional components: spirits, tea, citrus, sugar and spice. Each chapter of the book focuses on one of these elements, to help tailor punch to your palate. Drink Punch à la Romaine as served on the Titanic, or the bar's ever-popular milk punch (a creation that triggered the drink's revival at other bars across the capital), all served with beautiful edible flowers or elderberry garnishes. Afternoon tea gets a boozy twist and some cocktails have even been made into edible sweet versions by boutique alcoholic sweet company Smith & Sinclair. It's a far cry from the swill brought back from India to the UK by 17th-century sailors. But don't be surprised if you leave swaggering around like you've been on a boat. Once you get a taste for the punch, it's tough to tear yourself away. Hard-hitting drinking.

Address The London Edition, 10 Berners Street, W1T 3NP, +44 (0)20 7908 7949, www.editionhotels.com/london, punchroom.ldn@editionhotels.com | **Getting there** Tottenham Court Road (Central, Northern Lines) | **Hours** Mon–Sat 5pm–1am, Sun 5–11pm, afternoon tea reservations Fri–Sun 3–5pm | **Tip** While in the hotel, make a trip to Berners Tavern for phenomenal British cooking almost as old school as punch.

78__The Red Lion

Get a pizza the 'Action!'

Hollywood might be your bag, but haven't you heard? It's all about Ealing now. Come to The Red Lion to appreciate British movie-making in all its glory. Ealing Studios is just around the corner from this pub, which has stood on this site since the 1800s. The walls are covered with black-and-white stills from the movies and posters of *The Lavender Hill Mob*, *The Man in the White Suit* and *The Lady-killers*. Plus there's talk of stars having stood shoulder to shoulder at the bar in the studio's heyday.

Nowadays, you're more likely to find extras, editors and documentary-makers sharing off-set patter and industry chat over pints, since the studio is still in operation over the road. There's a heap of showbizzy American accents on show, that's for sure. But that's not to the exclusion of local families in with their kids for early evening dinners and students from the University of West London or Met Film School making a night of it. They cosy up in the front section of the pub, which has retained its wooden settles and booths and an old fire stove. But old school meets a modern, muted grey paint job and a small, light-filled conservatory at the back leading to a walled beer garden.

You'd be forgiven for thinking that you'd stepped onto the set of *The Godfather* rather than an Ealing Studios comedy, since the owners of neighbouring Santa Maria pizzeria have become land-lords of this Fuller's pub. Staff are young and attractive Italians with a fair few stallions in the mix, and they chat away in their native tongue between serving customers. Landlords Pasquale Chionchio and Angelo Ambrosio have joined up the kitchens and serve some of London's best pizzas fresh to the pub, as well as a menu of pub grub meets *cicchetti*. Swap your Scotch egg for a tempting lunch-time *manera*. That's an Italian-style sub, and it's what the British pub's been praying for all this time.

Address 13 Saint Mary's Road, W5 5RA, +44 (0)20 8567 2541, www.redlionealing.co.uk |
Getting there Ealing Broadway (Central, Circle, District Lines) | **Hours** Mon–Wed
11am–11pm, Thu–Sat 10am–midnight, Sun noon–11pm | **Tip** Ealing Studios don't currently offer tours, but head to the South Bank's BFI to brush up on your British film history.

79 _ Ridley Road Market Bar
Dalston's dirty disco shack

A cacophony of noise, colour and flavour has been synonymous with Ridley Road since the 1880s. The strip opposite Dalston Kingsland Station is where you'll find Ridley Road Market, with vendors selling fresh fruit and veg in among fabrics and electronics, backed by reggae tunes. Butchers here cater to a range of tastes, with a black market for rat meat uncovered by the press in 2012. But good things happened to this street in that year, too   Ridley Road Market Bar launched in an old shop space, bringing with it a modern interpretation of the area's energy.

The bar's beach-shack exterior is occupied by cool kids taking up the few seats on the terrace or a queue of bright young things snaking down the road. Inside, light fittings are fashioned from colanders for a bit of shanty chic and the wooden bar is painted in shocks of colour and decked with fairy lights, fruit and plant life all in a tangle. It's properly cheap here; tins of Red Stripe are half the price you'd get elsewhere, while cocktails cost around a fiver and include a suitably retro piña colada or a ginger mojito (topped with fresh mint sitting on the bar-top and mirroring the outside market). Pizzas are also cheap, with the Slice Girls' pun-heavy menu providing tongue-in-cheek sustenance. All the class is reserved for the dance floor, with chequered floor tiles, a shining mirror ball and palm-leafed plants lining the walls. Disco and pop attract a colourful crowd of late-night thrill-seekers, and at times it gets sweaty enough to fulfil the tropical brief.

With a potential fee hike putting the market traders' futures in jeopardy, it's great to see this fun-loving bar caring for its threatened community, proudly boasting the London Living Wage and giving back to local charity Dalston Bridge. Head along for the most fun you can have in London with none of that guilt the morning after.

Address 49 Ridley Road, E8 2NP, www.ridleyroadmarketbar.com, hello@ ridleyroadmarketbar.com | **Getting there** Dalston Kingsland (Overground) | **Hours** Tue 6pm–11pm, Wed 6pm–12.30am, Thu–Sat 6pm–2am, Sun 5–11pm | **Tip** For an equally good pizza fix late at night in Dalston, head over to Brooklyn-styled Voodoo Ray's (95 Kingsland High Street), open until 3am at weekends.

80 The Rolling Scones

'There is a light that never goes out'

Less bar, café and gallery, more madhouse, God's Own Junkyard is a singular setting for drinks in the electric glow of a neon company's private collection. The warehouse space out far northeast in Waltham-stow is filled from top to bottom with a vast spread of one-off neon artwork belonging to the Bracey family. Every inch of the room deserves your attention, from flashing sex shop signs to Union Jacks and semi-Art Deco items. And at the rear is The Rolling Scones, a café and bar in the midst of colour-filled wonder.

Chris Bracey began working in his father's neon company when the trade was geared towards fairground attractions. He brought creativity and a keen eye to proceedings when the company first had commissions from a then-thriving Soho sex scene. The iconic neon of Raymond's Revue was all Bracey's doing, with the star quoted to have kitted out '99 per cent of every sex establishment in Soho for 20 years'. As his notoriety grew, so too did the commissions – providing lights for everything from fashion shoots to film (*Eyes Wide Shut, Batman, Captain America*) and even art collaborations with the likes of David LaChapelle. Fans came to include Lady Gaga, Kate Moss and Grayson Perry.

God's Own Junkyard glowed beside the railway tracks in Waltham-stow until developments forced the collection to a new venue in 2013. An original bar was sourced from a local Victorian public house for The Rolling Scones, and behind it there's a stock of wine and tins of Red Stripe as well as a full range of beers from neighbouring Wild Card Brewery. And of course there are scones and snacks if savouring the atmosphere that bit longer.

Sadly, Chris Bracey passed away in 2014, but son Marcus along with Bracey's wife, Linda, continue the family legacy. Some of the signs tell the Junkyard story the best. One says: 'Where neon never dies'; and another: 'There is a light that never goes out'.

Address God's Own Junkyard, Unit 12, Ravenswood Industrial Estate, Shernhall Street, E17 9HQ, +44 (0)20 8521 8066, www.godsownjunkyard.co.uk, info@godsownjunkyard.co.uk | **Getting there** Walthamstow Central (Victoria Line, Overground) | **Hours** Fri & Sat 11am–9pm, Sun 11am–6pm | **Tip** Do a warehouse bar tour while in Walthamstow, with Wild Card Brewery and Mother's Ruin Gin Palace occupying spaces within the same industrial estate.

81 Royal Vauxhall Tavern
A right royal institution

Some question marks hang over this institution's future. Only recently, the company that owns Royal Vauxhall Tavern (RVT) was in attempts to sell the famed gay entertainment pub. But with backing from London Mayor Sadiq Khan, listed status and a new 20-year lease just signed by its landlord, it's hard – we hope – to see it disappearing. It's the first London venue to be given listed status because of its importance to the LGBTQ+ community after Sir Ian McKellen and Graham Norton backed the campaign. And as an asset of community value, it'll be difficult to make changes that would drastically alter its appearance or purpose. So there's clout behind the RVT Future group – made up of the pub's performers, promoters and punters – and its campaign for a community buyout.

And what a community it is. A pub has stood here since 1863 on the grounds of Vauxhall Pleasure Gardens, the centre of bohemian Victorian London. But the Tavern has been a queer pub since the 1950s when drag acts took to the bar top. As RVT's reputation grew, so did Vauxhall's for a gay night out, and The Tavern stayed at the centre with acts including an eight-year residency from Paul O'Grady's superstar alter ego, Lily Savage. Popular performance night Duckie has been here every Saturday for over twenty years, with London's Night Czar Amy Lamé at the helm. It also attracted star punters, with regular Freddie Mercury said to have smuggled Princess Diana into the pub in drag in '88 (nobody spotted royalty in among all the queens).

It wasn't just about the fun, with many using RVT as HQ during the AIDS crisis. It also faced famous police raids that became instrumental in changing the face of gay rights. It was the good times on stage that got these people through the bad. With so many iconic LGBTQ+ venues lost in London, it's more important than ever that this trailblazer stands tall for times to come.

Address 372 Kennington Lane, SE11 5HY, +44 (0)20 7820 1222, www.vauxhalltavern.com |
Getting there Vauxhall (Victoria Line) | **Hours** Mon–Thu 7pm–midnight, Fri 7pm–3am,
Sat 9pm–2am, Sun 2pm–2am | **Tip** The Eagle is an equally entertaining gay pub whose
cabaret and drag acts keep Vauxhall laughing.

82_ Ruby's
Ruby Tuesday, Wednesday, Thursday, Friday…

It started with Shoreditch. Then there was Hoxton. Then, in the early teens, Dalston was the epicentre of everything that was cool about the capital. One of the bars signaling the changes for the once-neglected part of town was Ruby's, doing so in its own unique way: via a daily-changing message on a cinema-style light box above its otherwise unmarked entrance.

A sign of the gentrified times, Ruby's name and light box come from the Chinese takeaway that used to be on this site, Ruby House 3. A location firm took over the townhouse and transformed it into a photography studio, but the owners' son, Tom Gibson, pushed to get a licence in the basement where the Chinese kitchen once resided. Clever him; it's quite the space. The walls are stripped to give an elegantly decaying look, rickety furniture and vintage lamps are set off-kilter and an opium-den-red hue (not quite ruby) is cast across the room. Rhubarb sours and spiced apple martinis are served in vintage glassware – gone are the jam jars and 1940s milk bottles that, like those wonky lampshades, soon became ubiquitous on the London drinking scene – placed on beer mats from around the world. It's a trendsetting yet unpretentious bar where you'll get a cocktail umbrella in your piña colada. As such, it's favoured by a cool crowd, with *Vogue* among the fashion rag fans.

Ruby's has even expanded to include a gold-walled, disco-esque lounge. Vietnamese food used to be served here (not Chinese takeaway, as you may have expected), but now the the lounge chooses to focus on wine and weekend revelry. Expect the disco look to spread across London like wildfire. That customisable message above the door varies – 'What is going on down there?' or 'God help us' the day after the 2016 US presidential election – but 'Nothing to see here' is perhaps one of the bar's most tongue-in-cheek and utterly inaccurate declarations.

Address 76 Stoke Newington Road, N16 7XB, www.rubysdalston.com,
hello@rubysdalston.com | Getting there Dalston Kingsland (Overground) | Hours Tue–Thu
6.30pm–midnight, Fri & Sat 6.30pm–2am | Tip The light box across the road is legit at Rio
Cinema. Head for indie films, selected blockbusters and screenings of old classics.

83__Rules

Conduct an affair with a little-known icon

Perhaps it's unlikely that a location billed as London's oldest restaurant should find a place here, but that may just be the beauty of Rules Cocktail Bar. With the noise surrounding the ancient dining room below – everyone from Clark Gable to Joan Collins has dined here – not many people are aware of the bar's existence.

Rules first opened in 1798, making it London's longest-surviving restaurant. It began life as an oyster bar and flourished into the restaurant known today for feasts of suet pudding. It's only changed ownership twice and even stayed open during the Blitz, given its reinforced structure and the rationed meals it served. The plush room with its fusty yet opulent look has appeared in *Downton Abbey* and in the novels of Evelyn Waugh and Graham Greene. But maybe they missed a trick not using upstairs for inspiration.

A staircase to the side leads to a boudoir-meets-country-club room. Dressed in red like a femme fatale and with double-ended chaises longues, it would suit the kind of encounter it was once used for when Edward VII and Lillie Langtry were conducting an affair up here; a portrait of the mistress now graces the wall in tribute. A frieze that borders the ceiling and depicts a fox-and-hound hunting scene contradicts that seductive air but keeps the landed gentry of London happy. Sure, you get some plummy accents, but most punters seem to be Yanks or shoppers resting their weary legs. Guests are greeted with friendly gesticulations, suited staff parade the room and deft hands work quietly behind a bar that's watched over by photos of the royal family. Martinis suit the occasion and are always stirred, never shaken.

Although there was a time when Rules – standing within church grounds – couldn't open on a Sunday, it's now the ideal setting on the day of the Lord, a peaceful bubble that serves one of the best Bloody Marys in London.

Address 34–35 Maiden Lane, WC2E 7LB, +44 (0)20 7836 5314, www.rules.co.uk, mike@rules.co.uk | Getting there Covent Garden (Piccadilly Line) | Hours Mon–Sat noon–midnight | Tip Actress and socialite Lillie Langtry would have probably enjoyed the French chic of Ladurée in Covent Garden Market, an adorable macaron shop and café first made famous in Paris.

84 The Running Horse
Well-groomed thoroughbred of a boozer

You can walk around Mayfair's historic squares and back alleys gasping for a pint. Gone are the establishments of yesteryear thanks to rising rents; hotel bars and member's clubs are mostly all that's left to quench your thirst. Luckily, Mayfair's oldest pub – here since 1738 – still stands after a makeover in 2013 that made it the area's most modern old-fashioned pub. A horseracing theme and wood-panelled appearance give the pub an undisputed British edge. This was once Davies Mews, an area occupied by livery stables and coach houses, and so the thoroughbred theme is anything but spurious. Horsey pictures on the walls are inspired by the work of Victorian photographer Eadweard Muybridge, ceramic beer pumps have traditional horse-and-hound illustrations, food is listed on a *Racing Post*-style paper and menu items include 'jockey whips' (aka chips).

Hereford's Chase Distillery is one of the backers of this gee-gee, with owner James Chase teaming up with Harvey Nichols' former bar manager Dominic Jacobs to find the right site for a cosy pub venture after the pair met at one of the distillery's tours. As such, it was the first UK pub to have Chase gin and vodka on the optics – don't miss the award-winning marmalade vodka or one of the best gin and tonics going. This also lends itself well to the pub's cocktail bar up above, The Whip. It's here that the theme gets frenzied, with rosettes, trophies, whips, saddles, racing stripes and a menu of juleps like the ones drunk at the Kentucky Derby every year.

In the past, The Running Horse attracted bankers and mining moguls, but nowadays you're just as likely to bump into established actors and Mayfair's cooler crowd. Crossrail developments have in many ways improved this pub, keeping it tucked out of sight from the Oxford Street masses. You'll probably get a seat, perhaps even a Chesterfield by the posh fireplace.

Address 50 Davies Street, W1K 5JE, +44 (0)20 7493 1275, www.therunninghorsemayfair.co.uk, info@therunninghorsemayfair.co.uk | **Getting there** Bond Street (Central, Jubilee Lines) | **Hours** Mon–Sat noon–midnight, Sun 11am–8pm | **Tip** Take a stroll down to Shepherd Market for more of Mayfair's Georgian taverns ranged around a historic square.

85__Sager + Wilde
A love affair with wine

You may know your Chardonnay from your Chablis, but what the hell's a Catarratto? Sager + Wilde is poised to answer the question, a bar bringing hard-to-find wines to the Hackney Road. The menu reads like a foreign language poem to the wine illiterate, but even if you're not one of the many oenophiles propping up the bar, there's no wine snobbery at this hip hangout. Staff share their passion or leave you be, their ability to read the situation as special as that Catarratto (it's a dry white from Sicily, in case you were wondering).

Love was the motivation behind Sager + Wilde, with married couple Michael Sager and Charlotte Wilde keen to spread their passion fresh from the fields of wine harvests in South America and from behind the bar in California, where they'd travelled together. The pair knew how hard it was to sample the grapes they'd been learning about without forking out for a bottle. It inspired them to buy up stock and sell it by the glass at lower mark-ups than found at restaurants. That's how their London pop-up Bird & Ballard was born, a hotly tipped opportunity to 'learn, taste and slurp' that lured in 250 guests on opening night.

Spurred on to go permanent, in 2013 they took over Edwardian pub The British Lion, a venue that used to host National Front meetings. St George's flags were supplanted by odds and ends from antique markets. Lamps from a Japanese tanker and vintage German station lights have been repurposed, while a bar top made from glass pavement lighting is as much of a talking point as the wine.

The pair may have since gone their separate ways, but Michael continues to steer the ship and love hasn't left the operation. In its first few years, the bar had served over 6,000 different wines, and the constant pouring continues. On any given night expect to see couples on date night or friends getting intimate with unheard-of grapes, oozing cheese toasties and attractive, attentive bar staff.

Address 193 Hackney Road, E2 8JL, +44 (0)20 8127 7330, www.sagerandwilde.com, hello@sagerandwilde.com | Getting there Hoxton (Overground) | Hours Mon–Wed 5pm–midnight, Thu & Fri 5pm–1am, Sat noon–1am, Sun noon–midnight | Tip Pore over your wine in more detail by booking a table at the bar's follow-up restaurant Sager + Wilde Paradise Row.

86 — The Salisbury Hotel

Star of the big screen

Few buildings are as imposing as this turn-of-the-century icon on the Harringay Ladder. Just up from the Turkish bakeries and barbers of Green Lanes stands this showy marvel on the suitably named Grand Parade. The Salisbury Hotel was built in 1898 and acts as a snapshot of the great pub boom of the time. Architect John Cathles Hill – the Scotsman responsible for a great number of buildings in the area – made this domed, four-storey glory (along with its twin, The Queens in Crouch End). Its name is highlighted across the middle of the building as well as in gorgeous ironwork above the door. Its cornices and columns command attention and its towering beauty is the pride of the neighbourhood. Modern picnic benches on the pavement are always packed with summer drinkers (despite the groaningly large space inside), so it's impossible to miss the place.

That's just as well, as The Salisbury's just-as-epic interior deserves attention too, especially after 2003 when Remarkable Restaurants carefully restored the then-unloved pub to glory. As befits the group's name, the pub grub's on point, especially the Salisbury burger (not quite as towering as the building). Libations are equally lip-smacking, with plenty of local ales to sample. But it's still the Salisbury's natural beauty that draws the most attention from visitors. Original fireplaces are stunning, old-fashioned mirrors glisten behind the bar and a billiards room at the rear now doubles as a function area. The saloon is the best: an island bar, black-and-white floor tiles and taxidermy in glass cases.

As such, it's little surprise that movie directors have selected The Salisbury as a film location, the pub acting most notably as the backdrop in Attenborough's *Chaplin* and Conenberg's *The Spider*. There are few pubs in London as deserving for a moment on the silver screen as this blockbuster boozer.

Address 1 Grand Parade, Green Lanes, Saint Ann's Road, N4 1JX, +44 (0)20 8800 9617, www.remarkablepubs.co.uk, salisbury@remarkablepubs.co.uk | Getting there Turnpike Lane (Piccadilly Line) | Hours Mon–Thu noon–11am, Fri 5pm–2am, Sat noon–2am, Sun noon–11am | Tip For eating that's just as ambitious, grab a set menu from one of many amazing Turkish restaurants on the Green Lanes stretch. Gökyüzü (26–27 Grand Parade) is a go-to for many.

87__Salon

Natural wine time

While a natural wine bar and bistro in the middle of a market might sound a bit more middle-aged than anything, Salon is actually spearheading one of London's coolest drinking movements. The restaurant began as a pop-up in 2012 before evolving to become a semi-permanent offering in Brixton's famous covered market. It's now here for good and has gradually expanded – proof that slow and steady definitely wins the race. While upstairs at Salon is dedicated to seasonal dining – and what good dining it is – it's the downstairs bar where it's at for the drinkers, extending out to the benches under heaters and in front of Salon's market-facing façade. And in 2017 came the opportunity for Salon to sprout a shop next door, flogging bottles of low-intervention wine, one of the venue's major passion points.

London's natural wine scene has been steadily fermenting, and there's no doubt that Salon has played a part in the drink's increasingly hip credentials. The last few years has seen the wine adopted as a party drink at east London jazz nights, all-day summer discos and the coolest music festivals outside of the capital. And at Salon, it's no different. Not only does the bar sell plenty of interesting drops by the glass produced by cool young winemakers from around the world, but it also throws some pretty wild parties.

The bar-restaurant's managing director Mark Gurney noticed an overlap in two of his favourite worlds. The wine lover and record label owner found that, just like him, a lot of his music industry friends had a deep passion for the grape. That was when Strictly Bangers was born, a monthly club night inside the wine shop where sommeliers, restaurant managers and general hospitality dons bring their record collection along for a night of curated tunes alongside the booze. The party often spills into Market Row and shows passersby just how cool wine can be.

Address 18 Market Row, SW9 8LD, +44 (0)20 7501 9152, www.salonbrixton.co.uk, info@ salonbrixton.co.uk | Getting there Brixton (Victoria Line) | Hours Tue–Fri noon–3pm & 6–11.30pm, Sat 10am–3pm & 6–11.30pm, Sun 10am–3pm | Tip Head to Peckham to enjoy even more of the grape stuff at Salon's sister restaurant Levan.

88__Satan's Whiskers

A devilishly deceptive dive bar

You'd hardly identify this as the best place for cocktails in east London from a cursory Google search. Take a look on Street View and you'll find graffiti, gig posters, some rusty old shutters and a blurry black-on-red paint job. And at night, the only sign of life is a scrawled neon sign that says 'Satan's Whiskers'. But go on, be a devil and step inside.

It used to be home to Lubanna, a jerk chicken joint just around the corner from Bethnal Green station, but now you're greeted with a classy, New York-style bar where the spiciest thing is the hip-hop soundtrack (think Rick Ross, Biggie and Outkast). It's related to east London pubs The Hemingway and The Hunter S (ch. 55), and like its brothers it breaks out the taxidermy. But unlike those pubs, stuffed critters strike cheeky poses with props like cocktail shakers and further decoration comes from vintage booze prints framed on the walls. That's right, it's all about the drinks here.

As with any decent dive, the best seats in the house are up at the bar. Cocktails are served by talented young staff who've moved from London's most upmarket hotels and speakeasies to be where the fun is, and they're treated like celebrities here with their names printed on the menu whenever they're working. They maintain a hip nonchalance about this and all the accolades rolling in, instead focusing on showing guests a damn good time.

The cocktail list changes daily and fruit is on display on ice for the freshest of garnishes. The bar churns out classics as well as inventive new recipes, including an award-winning Silver Pineapple, mixing Cuban white wine with rum, pineapple, lime and sugar. Satan's Whiskers even takes its name from a cocktail, a careful balance of gin, vermouth, orange, bitters and a splash of orange liqueur. It's elaborate yet simple, lively, and altogether original. Yep, that perfectly sums up this great little haunt.

Address 343 Cambridge Heath Road, E2 9RA, +44 (0)20 7739 8362, www.facebook.com/satanswhiskers | **Getting there** Bethnal Green (Central Line) | **Hours** Daily 5pm–midnight | **Tip** For more taxidermy fun, head up the road to the foot of Mare Street to find The Last Tuesday Society, a bar packed to the rafters with curiosities.

89 __ Scooter Caffè

Eccentric, Vespa-loving café-bar

If you're looking for Hell's Angels, you've come to the wrong place. This lovable hangout tucked away from the chaos of Waterloo station is all about the humble Vespa. Yet the atmosphere any night of the week is as roaring as a Harley Davidson as the joint moves seamlessly from espressos to espresso martinis.

Scooter Caffè began its life in 2000 as dedicated Vespa repair shop Scooterworks, where Kiwi owner Craig O'Dwyer would welcome Italian moped fanatics while they indulged in coffee from his vintage Faema machine. As the operation evolved and grew, new premises for the business were sought in Bermondsey, leaving Scooter Caffè to focus on its coffee-loving audience. Nowadays, the bar-café also roasts coffee and bakes indulgent cakes. But there's just as much of a focus on caffeine-free drinks and good times in the evenings.

It's not just the backstory that makes this place so special though; a multitude of quirks await newcomers. A candy-striped awning, neon lighting and benches outside make it pop on street level along Lower Marsh. But venture inside for an assault on the senses from twinkly fairy lights, vintage moped parts, a jumble of miscellany on the walls and a ceramic- and deck-chair-filled patio to the rear. Make your way down some precarious stairs to a musty and far more minimalist basement for a cosy catch-up over a negroni or another of the gin-based cocktails mixed at the bar.

A blend of customers, from students to tourists, flock in after dark – even on a Monday night you'll have to keep a keen eye out for one of those mismatched seats. But it's not just customers vying for a cosy spot. Scooter Caffè's own mog curls up without a care, despite the hum of happy chatter and '60s tunes. She's an exceptionally cute tabby cat, and the fact that she's named Bob only seems to chime with the venue's other adorable idiosyncrasies.

CAFFÈ

Please Mind

Address 132 Lower Marsh, SE1 7AE, +44 (0)20 7620 1421, www.facebook.com/
scootercaffe | **Getting there** Waterloo (National Rail, Bakerloo, Jubilee, Northern,
Waterloo & City Lines) | **Hours** Mon–Thu 8.30am–11pm, Fri 8.30am–midnight, Sat
10am–midnight, Sun 10am–11pm | **Tip** Come early evening for a pre-theatre drink then
check out The Vaults just off Lower Marsh for avant-garde and immersive productions.

90___Scout

Get wasted

Getting wasted in London has taken on new meaning, as many of the capital's standout bars have been putting sustainability on the agenda with minimum – even zero – waste policies. Leading the conscious charge is Scout, a bar that takes the planet and its resources as seriously as the drinking. The Hackney bar is from a pair of drink supremos. The first is Matt Whiley aka Talented Mr Fox. Whiley set up a bar consultancy under this guise after working across and establishing many of the city's best bars. And the second whizz is Rich Woods, aka The Cocktail Guy, who made his name creating drinks at the Heron Tower's swanky Duck & Waffle bar. At Scout, though, the focus is unique. The bar only uses produce from the British Isles on its menus, and goes by the motto: 'live off the land'. Scout was actually first established in Shoreditch by Whiley in 2017, but it closed and moved in 2018 with Woods helping him take the concept to the next level and to an even cooler east London audience.

Discover cocktails on a menu that changes daily in response to what's in season and which themes its sections around the UK's different ecosystems – from 'towns and cities' to 'forests and grasslands'. Drinks also include a list of house 'ferments' for *The Good Life* crowd, including fermented rhubarb served sparkling. In a similar vein, the bar brews its own beer using yeast cultivated on site – it's a frothy number, for sure. Even the snack menu approaches the theme of sustainability, with waste from the drink production process used to create bites to eat.

All wizardry takes place below ground in a metallic laboratory space filled with high-tech gadgetry from sous vide water baths to fermenting vats. But otherwise, the ground-floor bar is all minimal and modern Scandinavian chic, with clean lines and pine décor. An earthy setting for drinks to make you think about the planet.

Address 224 Graham Road, E8 1BP, +44 (0)20 8985 5128, www.scout.bar, hello@scout.
bar | Getting there Hackney Central (Overground) | Hours Wed & Thu 6pm–midnight,
Fri & Sat 5pm–midnight | Tip Try zero-waste dining at Cub in Hoxton. The clever concept
comes from Ryan Chetiyawardana aka Mr Lyan of Lyaness fame (ch. 62).

91_Seven Stars

...but two stars in particular

Roxy Beaujolais and Tom Paine sound like characters in *Chicago*. But they're associated with a pub in among historic Lincoln's Inn Fields. Spared by the Great Fire of London, Seven Stars has stood on Carey Street since 1602, allowing it to lay its claim – like many – as London's oldest pub. Long before it was serving the Royal Courts of Justice, it's said to have attracted Dutch sailors, its name homage to the seven Netherland provinces. In more recent history it catered to defendants at Carey Street's bankruptcy court, its location said to have helped coin the phrase 'on queer street' (meaning one was in financial dire straits). With the court now round the corner, Seven Stars is the only thing left on this road that's queer, a pinnacle of British eccentricity.

Beaujolais is the landlady. And if you don't spy her shock of pink hair, you'll see her in black-and-white snaps looking *très chic*. You'll also find posters for British courtroom comedies in honour of the local jurors, along with hops hanging from the walls and continental checked tablecloths. This matches a rustic menu of pâté, meatloaf and cheese and onion pie, a retro dinner-party streak from Beaujolais' prime as a '90s cookbook writer. She makes a mean dry martini, although most regulars – known by name – opt for French wine or Adnams ale. Her foodie leanings are spied from outside, with 'Soused herring and potato salad' written on the windows. Another window announces 'The Wig Box', since the pub expanded into the space once used as a shop for barristers sourcing headgear.

As for Tom Paine, well, he's no longer with us. Seven Stars' deceased mouser was a famed figure, a black cat who paraded the bar in an Elizabethan ruff. A poem on the wall is dedicated to him. He's had two successors since his departure in 2011 – Ray Brown and Peabody – who haven't quite had Tom Paine's panache in the ruff.

Address 53 Carey Street, WC2A 2JB, +44 (0)20 7242 8521, www.thesevenstars1602.co.uk | Getting there Chancery Lane (Central Line) | Hours Mon–Sat 11am–11pm, Sun noon–10.30pm | Tip Match the eccentricity by booking a game of tennis on outdoor lawns in Lincoln's Inn Fields, a surreal way to work out in among the high courts.

92___ The Ship

Riverside beers and a bit of brewing history

Young's pub group may be over 130-strong, but in the 1830s it was all about a brewery based in Wandsworth and a clutch of pubs in south-west London. Young's had taken over The Ram Brewery, which came to be the oldest British brewery in continuous operation, inextricably linking the area to beer. The brewery shut in 2006, so the closest you'll get to the group's humble beginnings is a trip to one of those early pubs close to former HQ. Set sail to The Ship; the riverside hostelry is a fine example of countryside chic in the capital, a stark contrast to the surrounding industrial plants and high-rise flats that dominate the riverbank. It's a relief to hear recent plans for a super sewer positioned here were vetoed.

The Ship first opened in 1786 and still shows hallmarks of those early days, particularly in its front snug where it's ideal to sup ale and pore over the papers, shielded from industrial life by frosted glass. You'll no doubt find your drink accompanied by patter from engaged and outgoing staff, who muse over the restorative powers of the pub's Scotch egg. A modern and light-filled conservatory is attached with pretty gastropub plates – and less elegant but ever-so-fitting dishes like fish and chips – arriving at tables ranged around a freestanding wood-burner. But the pub is probably best known for its river-facing drinking deck, a dominating spot by the Wandsworth Bridge. Large picnic tables are ideal for the inevitable groups of Hooray Henries that congregate at The Ship on rugby match days, while a 'burger shack' helps them pace themselves.

In 2016, Wandsworth became the first council in the UK to pass a bill protecting all of its pubs as community assets, making them the best-protected boozers in the land. With the loss of Young's Brewery and with the industrial state of play in the area, what sweet relief it is to know The Ship will stay loyal to the area's pubby roots despite the changing tides.

Address 41 Jews Row, SW18 1TB, +44 (0)20 8870 9667, www.theship.co.uk, ship@youngs.co.uk | Getting there Wandsworth Town (National Rail) | Hours Mon–Wed 11am–11pm, Thu–Sat 11am–midnight, Sun 11am–11pm | Tip The Alma in Wandsworth is another of Young's original fleet, and a beauty at that.

93__Slim Jim's Liquor Store
Rock 'n' roll bar with added bras

When Slim Jim's threw open its saloon doors in 2008, it was claiming to do so as London's first ever LA-style dive bar. It still fits the bill as a disreputable drinking den of sorts, with a simple black façade giving nothing away. Entry to this rock 'n' roll joint is only permitted to those dressed appropriately, but don't worry, it's a reverse door policy: strictly no suits allowed.

Inside, it's all about tattooed bar staff nonchalantly pouring from a hardcore range of spirits in a darkened room. Whisky bottles are stacked in rows up against the wall, but bourbon is king and beer from America's Captain Lawrence Brewing Co seals the US-dive-bar deal. Come during happy hour to sample two-for-one whisky sours and Manhattans and to take advantage of a deal on the bar's picklebacks (whisky chased with pickle juice, duh?). The dive bar stays open until 3am – a bit of a rarity in Islington – and the music keeps this place rocking that late. There's live music or a jukebox playing anthems from the likes of Zeppelin, Sabbath and Soundgarden, and dancing on the bar like you're in Coyote Ugly is practically encouraged. Perhaps this party spirit extends from Slim Jim's Irish ownership, with the family name 'Donnelly's' inside a neon shamrock on the wall.

Yet the talking point of Slim Jim's is the hundreds of bras hanging from the ceiling. Staff haven't shelled out on lady's undergarments but have had them thrust upon them instead. In the bar's early days, female customers were offered a bottle of fizz in return for a flash of their boobs or for handing over their bra. As the promotion took off, a bottle of booze became a Slim Jim's T-shirt, which in turn became a shot of that liquor (inflation, eh?). Liberated lady drinkers can still take advantage of the offer, throwing up all kinds of feminist arguments at the bar. To help soothe naysayers, management matches the price of each bra with a donation to support charity Breast Cancer Care. Naughty but nice, then.

Address 112 Upper Street, N1 1QN, +44 (0)20 7354 4364, www.slimjimsliquorstore.com, info@slimjimsliquorstore.com | **Getting there** Angel (Northern Line) | **Hours** Mon–Wed 4pm–2am, Thu–Sat 4pm–3am, Sun noon–1am | **Tip** For a similarly distressed décor, live music and a party attitude, head up Essex Road to the Queens Head, a pub with a fairly late licence to boot.

94_ Southampton Arms
Public house perfection (plus pork)

Faded portraits of Victorian characters, church pews for seats, dim lights, creaking floorboards, a cash-only bar and a (slightly humming) toilet outhouse for the gents. It's not sounding all that modern. Plus, the Southampton Arms' tell-it-as-it-is signage outside simply offers: 'ale, cider, meat'. But this modest Gospel Oak pub doesn't need to make contemporary gestures to convince that it's one of London's finest places for a pint.

Shining white tiles draw your eye to the bar, where all the modern flourishes come into play. Landlord Peter Holt turned his attention to the beer when taking on the lease of this failing Courage pub in 2009. He championed independent UK breweries unlike anyone had done in the capital. The imitators have come thick and fast since – the pub even makes note of a particular Stoke Newington rival on its website – but it remains London's only ale and cider house strictly dedicated to UK indies. Ten hand-pulls are given over to ales, while a further eight pour English and Welsh ciders, all of which come in dimpled jugs for an old-fashioned drink to match the semi-Dickensian setting. And that aforementioned 'meat' is classic pub fare with piggy snacks including sausage rolls, pork pies, crackling, Scotch eggs and the Southampton's much-loved hot pork baps.

Jazz records spin from a player at the bar, or there's weekly piano sessions (more jazz, with the occasional trumpet accompanist). People vie for a spot by the open fire, especially if they've brought along the papers and their pooch (although any dogs in tow must get along with the pub's cats, Pork Pie and Scratchings). Otherwise, there's the heated garden open until 10pm (at which point a leopard will be released, if the pub's messaging is to be believed). With all that in mind, it's hardly a surprise that punters struggle for a table on a drizzly Sunday. There's no place quite as warming.

Address 139 Highgate Road, NW5 1LE, www.thesouthamptonarms.co.uk | Getting there Gospel Oak (Overground) | Hours Mon–Sat noon–midnight, Sun noon–10.30pm | Tip Feel less guilty about tucking into pork and pints with a trip to Hampstead Heath's outdoor swimming ponds beforehand (perhaps not after, though).

95 __ Spaniards Inn

Haunted olde-worlde inn

Not much is Spanish about this traditional public house at the uppermost heights of Hampstead's hilly Spaniards Road. In fact, it's steeped in history and shrouded in the kind of folklore that could only come out of years of banter over pints down the pub. The Spaniards, first established around 1585, was once a coaching inn that gave shelter to the likes of Bryon, Shelley and Keats. It's little surprise, then, that the pub features in Bram Stoker's *Dracula* and Dickens' *The Pickwick Papers*.

It is also rumoured to have offered shelter to glamorised highwayman Dick Turpin. Even more fantastical, if regulars are to be believed, the pub is haunted by a number of ghosts, the most common sighting being a Spaniard who lost his life in a duel of love at the pub. But a mysterious woman in white has also been spotted by north Londoners, as well as the spectre of Dick Turpin, who's rumoured to roam the road outside.

If this level of London history doesn't have you pining for a pint at The Spaniards, the setting will surely lure you in, with low oak-clad ceilings and walls, creaking floorboards and a stunning Heath-side location. It's like a country pub at the edge of north London, with a massive beer garden to boot. And snug rooms off to the side of the main bar certainly offer an olde-worlde feel straight out of a Dickens novel (aptly so), even if ghosts from the past don't make an appearance.

Nowadays, you're more likely to be greeted by adorable dogs than ghoulish apparitions, anyway. The Spaniards attracts hounds by the dozen with dog walkers seeking it out after a brisk jaunt across the Heath. Modern-day bar staff happily provide a bowl of water for thirsty pooches. In keeping with the ghostly theme, the pub even hosts a fancy dress parade for pups every Halloween, which can attract quite the turnout. What's not to like about pugs dressed as pumpkins?

Address Spaniards Road, NW3 7JJ, +44 (0)20 8732 8406, www.thespaniardshampstead.co.uk | Getting there Hampstead (Northern Line) | Hours Mon–Sat noon–11pm, Sun noon–10.30pm | Tip For even more history in leafy surrounds, take a stroll around neighbouring stately home Kenwood House.

96 Spiritland

Get into the groove

New to the scene in 2016, Spiritland immediately became known as a muso's hangout – that place where you'd have regular sightings of music industry types waving to acquaintances they've spied across the room. That's because it's London's first 'listening bar', which makes it sound far more wanky than it actually is. What it means is a bar where one of the main attractions is actually the sound system, and where what's on the speakers is of just as much importance as the speaker itself.

Paul Noble was the man with the idea, having taken inspiration from Japan. He kitted out the space with custom-built speakers that cost a small fortune, and which were tested and tweaked using classical music. Mixers, turntables and top-of-the-range hi-fi gear make this one of the most advanced audio systems in the capital. The bar combines high-end audio with a broad music policy. But forget the dancing; this is a 'deep listening experience'. As such, find the DJ to the side of the room as opposed to centre stage.

Every evening, Spiritland plays one album from start to finish, so you can hear some of your best-loved hits in a whole new way while sipping on sake, beers served in schooner measures and cocktails named after songs. Wine is even high-fidelity, with grapes listed by their level of skin contact. Producers and DJs run takeovers each day, playing tunes on their preferred medium – it's not all about vinyl – while musician Q&As and album launches are a regular fixture. There's a production studio to the side made to look like a '50s radio booth and from which Spiritland can run broadcasts. The venue even has its own record and tech store, selling hefty headphones and turntables. The Japanese look and unique, out-of-this-world feel of the experience can have you thinking you're starring in *Lost in Translation*. What isn't lost among this crowd though is the emotion of music powered through tech.

Address 9–10 Stable Street, N1C 4AB, www.spiritland.com, info@spiritland.com | Getting there King's Cross (Circle, Hammersmith & City, Metropolitan, Northern, Piccadilly, Victoria Lines) | Hours Mon & Tue 8am–midnight, Wed–Sat 8am–1.30am, Sun 10am–10pm | Tip Cult Indian restaurant Dishoom next door is as much of an assault on the senses, if you can stand the queue to get in.

97__ The Spread Eagle

London's first fully vegan pub

From the drinks right down to the candles, every last detail at The Spread Eagle is animal-free. The Homerton spot opened in 2018 as London's first fully vegan pub at a time when veganism was in the ascendance. Not only does the smart-looking boozer produce food and drink that keeps vegans in mind, but the whole pub's ethos is based around the animal-free philosophy. And yet, it's far from the kind of hippyish place that might spring to mind; there's no tie-dye-wearing staff, no wind chime-heavy décor and no psytrance soundtrack. The Spread Eagle and its founders have helped show the capital that veganism doesn't have to be that way at all. The pub looks like any trendy east London watering hole, kitted out in smart dark blues, with a striking central bar and with shelves fit to bursting with swiss cheese plants and twisting vines.

One of the pub's founders is Meriel Armitage, also the genius behind Club Mexicana, a vegan food stall that had previously made its name flogging Mexican grub at London street food markets and UK music festivals. The beer-battered 'tofish' tacos are a revelation, and they're now available to buy at the pub, alongside MFC (Mexican-fried chick'n) and nachos loaded with imitation chorizo and vegan 'cheez'. It's genuinely remarkable what they can do with a jackfruit here. And as for the drinks, delicious sour cocktails cleverly get the required froth not from egg whites but from aquafaba (chickpea water). And all the beer and wine is vegan, too (you might be surprised by how many of your usual pints aren't).

The rest is all standard east London fare – from quiz nights to club nights to bloody marys the morning after (made with vegan worcester sauce, don't worry). And dogs are totally welcome – it's not *completely* animal-free! So head to this plant-based pub when you're after some feel-good drinking – although there's still no guarantee you'll get away without a hangover the next day.

Address 224 Homerton High Street, E9 6AS, +44 (0)20 8985 0400, www.thespreadeaglelondon.co.uk, hello@thespreadeaglelondon.co.uk | **Getting there** Homerton (Overground Lines) | **Hours** Mon–Thu 4–11pm, Fri 4pm–1am, Sat noon–2am, Sun noon–10.30pm | **Tip** For more plant-based grub with a cult-like status, check out Temple of Seitan on Hackney's Morning Lane, London's first vegan fried chicken shop.

98__ Stein's

Beer on the river? It could be wurst

You may get the sense you're in another city when you venture down south to Richmond, where couples rent rowboats on the river and tourists take in the countryside sights after a jaunt around Kew Gardens. But a visit to Stein's will have you feeling like you're in a different country. This German beer garden is a Bavarian bash on the banks of the Thames.

Owners Bele and Reinhard Weiss were pining for the outdoor drinking spots they'd left behind in Munich, so when a graffiti-covered ice cream hut on the banks in Richmond caught Reinhard's eye he had to enquire. Alas, it seemed the Weisses had acted too late, as it had already been sold. But imagine the *schadenfreude* when a year later they received a call letting them know the plans for the building had fallen through and the hut was theirs for the taking. By 2004, the couple had turned the shack into a thriving Bavarian kitchen-bar.

Place your beer order at one hut window and collect from another, find a space at a communal wooden bench – many sheltered by sturdy blue parasols and warmed by patio heaters – and let the fun begin. They're pouring classic Erdinger Weissbier and the authenticity attracts a smattering of Germans, many drawn in by the sausage. A broad menu includes *currywurst* and *bratwurst* served with a bread bun or with piles of mashed potato on the side. Or there's schnitzel for the bigger appetites. The formula has been so successful that a second cosy beer lodge arrived in Kingston shortly after.

Leave the lederhosen at home, since it's far more sedate than your average Oktoberfest party. Perhaps it's the raucous connotations of a German beer garden that has led to signage stating that Stein's is 'a family restaurant'. And due to the venue's licence, you'll need to order food if you're intent on browsing the beer selection. So go on, Rhine and dine by the Thames.

Address Richmond Towpath, TW10 6UX, +44 (0)20 8948 8189, www.stein-s.com, richmond@stein-s.com | **Getting there** Richmond (District Line, National Rail) | **Hours** (All weather-dependent) summer: daily noon–10pm, winter: Wed–Sun noon–dusk (4–6pm) | **Tip** Find shelter with your sausage at the second branch of Stein's on Kingston's High Street.

99__Sun Tavern

Strong drinks, low lights, good times

What may have been a menacing hangout filled with East End boxers (see the Salmon and Ball across the road for reference) has turned its gaze to Irish mischief and misdemeanours. The Sun Tavern has the largest stock of poitín in London, a historic Irish grain spirit only legalised in 1997. The bar stocks around 20 different varieties, no mean feat given the heavy taxation on imports as well as the drink's outlaw status until relatively recently. The Sun Tavern educates poitín virgins with regular tastings and you can try it by the glass or in cocktails. If that's a little left field for your tastes, the bar does hard liquor in the form of whisky at knocked-down prices on Whisky Wednesdays. Otherwise, it's about breweries within a five-mile radius, with 'local heroes' championed on regularly changing tap lines. Make it even more local by asking them to bottle some as a takeaway.

A revamp in 2014 saw some of The Sun's original features restored from its 1851 beginnings, including exterior tiles and artfully crumbling brickwork. Inside, walls are stripped and distressed for even more of that ancient-inn atmosphere. The somewhat piratey 'Tavern' name fits this new image, as does the punch menu, with drinks strong enough to suit the high seas served in metallic tankards. This may make The Sun Tavern sound old fashioned, but it's likely one of the edgiest establishments in the area, a follow-up to Aldgate speakeasy Discount Suit Company that shares a similar low-lit look. The Tavern stays modern with Venetian blinds, a copper-topped bar and red leather stools, although they're hard to see in barely-there candlelight.

Worried about your state after several rounds of poitín in the dark? The bar's toilets play soothing whale noises and a cardboard sign in lieu of a mirror reassuringly states: 'You look fine'. That Irish sense of humour should get you every time.

Address 441 Bethnal Green Road, E2 0AN, +44 (0)20 7739 4097, www.thesuntavern.co.uk | **Getting there** Bethnal Green (Central Line) | **Hours** Mon–Wed noon–midnight, Thu–Sat noon–1am, Sun noon–midnight | **Tip** Those East End boxers probably liked G. Kelly too, a classic pie and mash shop on Bethnal Green Road since 1915.

100__Swift

Make it more than a swift one

Open any guidebook to drinking in London and you'll find Nightjar, a 'secret' bar just off the Silicon Roundabout that defined the speak-easy movement when it discreetly opened its unmarked doors in 2010. Fast-forward six years to find its owners still shaping the scene, but in a pared-back, gimmick-free way at Swift in Soho. Maybe that's because husband-and-wife team Edmund Weil and Rosie Stimpson teamed up with peers and newlyweds Bobby Hiddleston and Mia Johansson to bring this bar to life. The latter duo have experience at some of London's best watering holes as well as New York's Dead Rabbit, often named the best bar in the world. That's one hell of a collective CV.

Swift's concept is simple; a bar with perching room only and no table service, where you can drop in for a quick but expert drink – be it a pre-prandial, nightcap or something in between. It's lit up like a Hollywood dressing room, with naked light bulbs running the ceiling and 'Champagne' and 'aperitivos' written in light boxes up on high. It's simple yet sophisticated, as are the drinks; a prosecco-based cocktail amped up with lemon sorbet, a Bloody Mary juiced to order.

If you do feel like resting your legs, the basement is a great place in which to do so. And that's not just because it looks the part, all dimly lit, Art Deco and brooding. It also has a 'whisky library' to explore stocking over 130 bottles of scotch plus many more drams from around the world. The lengthier list of cocktails in the downstairs bar relies heavily on dark spirits, whisky obviously included, so it's a great spot to get more serious, and an unbeatable spot for an Irish coffee. And just to add to the atmosphere, you'll find a piano in among the ottoman chairs and semi-circular booths, with live blues and jazz on Fridays and Saturdays – much like at Nightjar. Forget the swift half and swoop in wholeheartedly to this beaut little birdie.

Address 12 Old Compton Street, W1D 4TQ, +44 (0)20 7437 7820, www.barswift.com, info@barswift.com | Getting there Tottenham Court Road (Central, Northern Lines) | Hours Mon–Sat 3pm–midnight, Sun 3–10.30pm | Tip Check out Swift's half-sister bar, Oriole, by Smithfield Market, with one of the flashiest bar designs going and run by the Nightjar team.

101__Sylvan Post
First class pub

Make an express trip southeast for a spot of quirky drinking at the Sylvan Post. The former Forest Hill Post Office from the 1960s is part pub, part shrine-to-Royal-Mail. First class, second class and worldwide post boxes remain on the exterior as a clue to the building's old purpose. But once inside it's hard to hide from the origins of this unassuming local.

A minimal interior almost comes across as a glimpse behind the Berlin Wall with its low-ceiling, low-impact '60s look, linoleum floors and Formica tables. But the themed embellishments come thick and fast once you start to observe your surroundings. Commemorative stamps, telegrams and postcards are mounted on every last inch of wall. Read lingering love notes, hurried notices and fond well-wishes from far off lands while you wait for your pint. The bar is made from an old service counter and exchanges money for suds instead of stamps. And what once acted as a safe for precious cargo has now been converted into a cosy snug for private libations.

Running with a theme like this isn't entirely original. The pub group behind the Sylvan Post – Antic London – has form in transforming community buildings into boozers. Effra Social in Brixton is an old Conservative club now filled with the young and liberal, Balham Bowls Club sticks to its sporting roots while locals in Deptford were up in arms when the Job Centre opened, somewhat trivialising the deprived area's gentrification. But the Sylvan Post is one of the more tasteful renovations and one that Forest Hill has taken to heart, with a packed-out pub for Sundays' roasts and delivering the goods on a Monday with a real ale club that sees pints served just under the cost of a first class parcel. If you buy five pints, you get the sixth one for free, with guests getting their loyalty cards stamped by the staff. Can you see what they did there?

Address 24–28 Dartmouth Road, SE23 3XU, +44 (0)20 8291 5712, www.sylvanpost.com | Getting there Forest Hill (Overground) | Hours Mon–Thu 4–11pm, Fri 4pm–midnight, Sat noon–midnight, Sun noon–11pm | Tip Don't miss a trip to the Horniman Museum to see a local celebrity: a large stuffed walrus.

102 Tamesis Dock

A boat that rocks

On a grey stretch of Vauxhall where traffic rushes by and the Thames laps murkily against the embankment, this beauty of a barge is a beacon of light, its red, green and yellow colours bobbing about like a Rastafarian flag at a reggae concert. There's no gangplank, but a permanent shaky ramp from the roadside places seafaring drinkers onto a deck split in two and loaded with picnic benches. Here punters sip on pints or tuck into decent pub grub, with views across the river and the Houses of Parliament on the horizon. There's a bar immediately as you enter the boat's low-ceilinged inner sanctum, a dark space with light scattering through portholes as staff pour continental lagers and double-measure rums for the pirate wannabees. From here you can peer down into the belly of the boat, where bands and DJs make waves.

In 2008, this beautiful 1930s Dutch barge took on her current identity, but her original name is *The Anna G* and she once carried the rather demure title of *The English Maid*. Her current guise must be the most fitting; the good-time feel of this good ship echoes the very purpose she was built for: shuttling Champagne from Paris back to the Netherlands. She served her time in World War II as a transportation vehicle in Paris and was laid to rest soon after, before moving to Great Britain in the '80s to begin her life as a party boat, first down south and then in London.

And that merrymaking reputation hasn't slipped. Her success has even meant that another ship has recently joined the fleet, with the owners reuniting *The Anna G* with a sister boat from the Netherlands – *Battersea Barge* based further down the Thames. At night, twinkling string lights attached to the rigging make the deck on Tamesis Dock even more appetising – she's aided many a first date and even marriage proposals. So prepare your sea legs for a night to remember.

Address Albert Embankment, SE1 7TP, +44 (0)20 7582 1066, www.tdock.co.uk, ahoy@tdock.co.uk | **Getting there** Vauxhall (Victoria Line) | **Hours** Mon–Wed 11.30am–midnight, Thu & Fri 11.30–1am, Sat 10.30–1am, Sun 10.30am–midnight | **Tip** Across the Thames towards Embankment you'll find the *PS Tattershall Castle*, a floating steamboat bar for slightly more civilised drinking.

103 — The Tankard
Chaplin's old boozer turned beer pub

The owner and visionary behind the UK's ever-growing Draft House chain Charlie McVeigh was the first landlord to serve Sambrooks Wandle ale – a name now synonymous with good drinking – when he set up his Battersea pub the Westbridge. This beer-forward attitude was carried across to the core of the first Draft House in Battersea in 2009. Fast-forward to 2017 and The Tankard joined a 12-strong fleet of UK pubs in McVeigh's family. These bars call themselves the 'home of the third', serving drinks in third-of-pint measures to allow customers to sample more international keg beers without getting too squiffy. But what makes this Kennington outlet unique?

Well, Charlie Chaplin has something to do with it. The slapstick hero spent his childhood bouncing around the pubs of Kennington Road, often searching for his alcoholic father. The Tankard was one such spot his dad would frequent, and it was here that Chaplin drew inspiration for the comedy characters he'd later play. Inside the modern-day Tankard, the pub makes subtle references to The Little Tramp – from movie posters to illustrations. And the red-and-black décor harks back to the area's music hall heyday, since Chaplin's father had been a star of its stages.

The pub also overlooked the infamous Bethlem Psychiatric Hospital (known colloquially as 'Bedlam' – yes, that's where the word comes from – and now the site of the Imperial War Museum). It's said a roof terrace was built to accommodate nosey parkers keen to get a peek over the hospital's walls. You would never cotton on to this terrace's sinister origins, though, thanks to festoon lights and wooden pergolas making the space look so pretty.

So those into their booze should prioritise a trip to this branch of Draft House, a forward-thinking beer bar that doesn't rely on its iconic Victorian history, but brings out the best of it instead. No slapstick required.

Address 111 Kennington Road, SE11 6SF, +44 (0)20 7582 6685, www.drafthouse.co.uk |
Getting there Hoxton (Overground Lines) | **Hours** Mon–Thu noon–11pm, Fri & Sat
noon–midnight, Sun noon–10.30pm | **Tip** Have yourself a Chaplin pub crawl along the
Kennington Road. The Three Stags is where the star of the silver screen last saw his father
alive, and it now has its own 'Chaplin Corner'.

104__Tayēr + Elementary

Cocktails as cool as they come... frozen

Eastern European hip hop in the air, utility-aproned staff and katsu sandos (a Japanese take on a pork sarnie) for bar snacks: there's no denying that this two-part bar just off the Silicon Roundabout is as cool as they come. And it's been dreamed up by two of the international bar community's biggest names – Alex Kratena and Monica Berg. Kratena was head bartender at London's Artesian from 2012 to 2015, when it was consistently voted the best bar in the world. And Berg has made her name in bartending and consultancy work across Oslo and London. They're a powerful pair, and their first bar is proof of that fact.

For this epic collaboration, an old post office has been divvied up into two bar spaces. At the front is Elementary, a casual place to slip in for a drink any time of day – be that a frozen coffee cocktail, an iconic One-Sip Martini (served in a shot glass) or just a perfectly poured cold beer. They have cocktails on tap here, so service is speedy whatever you plump for. But Tayēr at the back is a little bit of magic, its name derived from the Spanish word for workshop, *taller*. Here, there's a square-shaped bar that closes in on a central metallic workstation, all set underneath exposed ceiling ducts. The rest of the room is all mid-century furniture, with sous-vide bags and ingredients casually left on the side. It's unlike any other bar layout in London, a bit science-lab-meets-Scandi-living-room. And yet somehow, it works so very well.

Drink from a menu that changes with the seasons and with the same regularity as the dishes at a farm-to-table restaurant (they describe their approach to the elements in their drinks as 'hyper-local'), using cheffy techniques to create in-house ingredients and showcasing the pair's own range of Muyu liqueurs. The results are dazzling cocktails that have the kind of lingeringly long finish you'd find with a fine wine. It's anything but elementary.

Address 152 Old Street, EC1V 9BW, www.tayer-elementary.com, cheers@tayer-elementary.com | **Getting there** Old Street (Northern Line and National Rail) | **Hours** Mon–Sat 11.30am–midnight | **Tip** Get another taste of that legendary pork sandwich over at Arcade Food Theatre, where Tayēr + Elementary's resident chef team Tā Tā Eatery have a stall under the name of Tōu that's dedicated to the katsu sando.

105_ Three Sheets

…and two brothers

Set up by two seemingly laidback Northerners, Three Sheets has become one of the drink industry's favoured hangouts, with brothers Max and Noel Venning now two of the bar world's brightest stars. But don't expect anything lofty at Three Sheets. This Dalston local stays down-to-earth despite the accolades.

Max spied the space was for sale while he was working nearby for the Drink Factory, a consultancy behind a number bars, including Bar Termini (ch. 7). They put in an offer, and in 2016 Noel moved down from Manchester to open Three Sheets (originally named 'Between the Sheets', a slightly naff cocktail reference) with his brother. It's a teeny room with flashes of moss green and bare brick, plus a couple of marble-topped tables for two and a nook at the back for bigger groups. But you'll want to be near the bar for some of that northern hospitality, and for a view on some of the cleverest cocktails in town.

The Brothers Venning brought with them a whole new approach that has rapidly become the way to drink in London: simple glassware, minimal garnishes and a cocktail list peppered with hot takes on the classics, many of which are pre-batched before service (they've even written a book on the subject). This formula might not sound revolutionary, but the flavours are phenomenal; and they might be pre-batched, but some of these drinks are days in the making.

Each one riffs on key ingredients, upping the ante of your favourite cocktail's flavour profile. As such, the Cosmo is a fruity pink drink with extra juiciness from fermented cranberries. And the french 75 contains none of the signature drink's fizzy wine – yet through carbonation, it still sparkles in your glass as it's poured at the table from a champagne bottle. Three Sheets is a family operation, but their offerings are nothing like the drinks you'd be having at home. The Venning's cocktails are out of this world.

Address 510b Kingsland Road, E8 4AB, +44 (0)7718 648771, www.threesheets-bar.com, info@threesheets-bar.com | Getting there Dalston Junction (Overground Lines) | Hours Daily 5pm–12.45am | Tip The Venning Brothers have branched out beyond cocktails now, opening a bistro and natural wine bar towards Finsbury Park named Top Cuvée.

106_ Trailer Happiness

If you like piña coladas…

In TV's *Mad Men*, Don Draper's wife shacks up in a Los Angeles Laurel Canyon bungalow a bit like this basement bar in Notting Hill. Imagine a late-'60s swinger's pad with a hint of beachy good vibrations, and you're practically there. A swirly carpet dresses the ground and low armchairs sit around mid-century coffee tables, but don't expect them to wheel across the drinks cabinet for an old fashioned. Because where '60s living room ends, Polynesian chic begins, with tropical flower arrangements and pineapple-shaped vessels dressing the bar, beaded curtains sectioning off the bathrooms and Tretchikoff prints depicting mysterious girls on the walls. It would be pure class if it weren't for the waxwork babe at the entrance in a grass skirt, floral lei and little else, but that's just the bar expressing its cheeky Tiki side.

Trailer Happiness has been wearing this look very well since 2003, when serial bar founder Jonathan Downey came up with a concept to suit west London. The idea was a metrosexual surfer's bachelor pad without any of the Tiki tackiness seen in other establishments. It's since been tweaked and toyed with, but much remains the same at one of London's longest-standing themed bars, now under the steer of local legend Sly Augustin – a fan of Trailer H for years.

Unsurprisingly, rum features heavily, doled out by approachable staff in Hawaiian-print shirts to dolled-up, twenty-something Notting Hillbillies. Most drinks come in traditional Tiki totem mugs, but look out for piña coladas in pineapples, flame-topped cocktails and even volcanoes erupting molten 'lava'. Rum Club traditionally runs on the first Monday of the month, where a brand ambassador or booze expert talks enthusiasts through the sugar cane spirit. And any other day of the week you might find the bar honouring a significant figure in rum's twisted history. Say 'aloha' to island living.

Address 177 Portobello Road, W11 2DY, +44 (0)20 7041 9833, www.trailerhappiness.com, reservations@trailerh.com | **Getting there** Ladbroke Grove (Circle, Hammersmith & City Lines) | **Hours** Mon–Wed 5pm–midnight, Thu 5pm–12.30am, Fri & Sat 5pm–1am, Sun 5pm–midnight | **Tip** Carry on the west London rum party. Cottons Caribbean restaurant along Notting Hill Gate describes itself as Carnival all year long, and it boasts a 250-strong rum list at its bar.

107__ Troubadour

Still rockin', sort of

'The password for the Wi-Fi is "bobdylan" all lower case,' staff tell customers making Troubadour their daytime base. So this Chelsea icon isn't as rock 'n' roll as in its heyday, but the password's definitely a clue to its heritage. The Brompton Road coffee house, bar and bistro with a quasi-medieval look that chimes with its name was a magnet for the free-spirited musicians, poets and painters of the area in the swinging '60s, and its basement stage hosted Jimi Hendrix, Paul Simon, Sammy Davis Jr – and, of course, Bob.

Folk music and poetic goings-on took off not long after it opened in 1954, which lured in Dylan, making his first mark on London here. During the capital's second wave coffee revolution, it acted as a centre of culture, conversation and bohemian life. Modest, folky beginnings and Monday night poetry readings grew to Ban the Bomb and Black Panther meet-ups. The first edition of *Private Eye* was even written and distributed here. Music became more renegade too, with the Rolling Stones stopping by for solo performances and Led Zeppelin holding impromptu post-stadium comedown gigs in the basement.

To this day, below ground marks the spot for rock 'n' roll, but a noise abatement issue has put Troubadour in jeopardy, and rents are rising. The bar went into administration in 2015 but has had backing from an existing shareholder to keep the legend alive. What remains is a more sedate spot for drinking, with American accents filling the air and steak frites and merlot Mondays. But it's also an atmosphere that echoes of past shenanigans. The look is creaking, from rusty old banjos and bric-a-brac on the ceiling and a magnificent hand-carved swing door at the entrance, to sparkling vintage café mirrors. There's definitely a buzz in the air of what might have happened here. Just visit the elaborate, be-fountained unisex toilets and let the mind wander.

Address 263–267 Old Brompton Road, SW5 9JA, +44 (0)20 7341 6333, www.troubadourlondon.com, manager@troubadour.co.uk | Getting there West Brompton (District Line, Overground) | Hours Mon–Sat 8.30am–midnight, Sun 8.30am–11.30pm, open until 2.30am on selected club nights | Tip Nam Long Le Shaker is another old-school institution in the area. This one invented the famous Flaming Ferrari, a champagne cocktail served on fire.

108_Unwined

A grape night out

It's a very London story: the pop-up that goes permanent, with a little help from crowdfunding. Unwined in Tooting began its life as roaming wine-themed event A Grape Night In, which came to people's homes but soon evolved to a pop-up party in quirky London venues. Friends Laura Aitken and Kiki Evans met as staff at Jamie Oliver's restaurant Fifteen, where they discovered a shared love for world wines. They decided to take their passion to a wider audience, sourcing bottles from interesting growers or regions with a fascinating history. For these passionate ladies, it was all about retelling that story and finding a new way to talk about plonk – away from the pomp.

As an audience grew for A Grape Night In, the idea of finding a permanent space felt like a no-brainer. So three years on from the start of the pop-up, Unwined was born in 2015. Wine bottles are used for light fittings, a cork-topped tasting table takes up most of the space, and a 'family tree' on the wall name-checks all the investors who helped make the bar happen. Somehow, the ever-changing nature of a pop-up is still present, with the clever pair showcasing eight wines per month to chime with topical themes – International Women's Day sees a light shone on female wine producers, for example, with bespoke decorations made to match each theme by shop supervisor and artist, Consuelo Celluzzi. To complement the vino, Laura and Kiki invite a different chef into the kitchen each month and ask them to create a menu to match with the wines, a nice reverse of the standardised norm.

You'll find this rustic, ramshackle wooden bar within just as ramshackle a building, Tooting Market. The old-school covered market is filled with local curiosities – from fortunetellers and sari shops to stalls selling fish heads and falafel wraps. It's great to see Unwined adding a new niche into the mix.

Address 16A Tooting Market, 21–23 Tooting High Street, SW17 0SN, +44 (0)20 3286 4631, www.agrapenightin.co.uk | Getting there Tooting Broadway (Northern Line) | Hours Tue 3–10pm, Wed–Sat 11am–11pm, Sun 11am–5.30pm | Tip Craft Tooting is a cute bottle shop within the market shining a light on craft beers in the same way that Unwined does on vino.

109__WC

A setting sprinkled with unique touches

In most circles, WC stands for one thing only. But this Clapham WC does more than rescue those caught short on the Common. It in fact does a mean trade in wine and charcuterie (W and C, geddit?). And it just so happens to be housed in an Edwardian public toilet at the foot of Clapham Common station.

Friends and locals Andy Bell and Jayke Mangion spent two years remodelling the underground space after the council awarded them the project, beating competition from around 450 other applicants. This former public lavatory had been condemned for use, with dangerous structural issues and leaks for Bell and Mangion to contend with. But with two years of TLC, WC was born. And what TLC it was, with as many original aspects from the toilet repurposed in furniture, fixtures and fittings (and carefully sanitised, we're promised!). So you'll find cubicle doors transformed into tables, mosaic tiling along the walls, original skylights intact and the attendant's box as the bar.

And what about the toilets? Here they've kept old-fashioned urinals and added pictures of pin-ups to the walls for peep-show-style entertainment. Meanwhile the ladies' cubicle has been decorated with cheeky 'love letters' that were discovered tucked behind tiles when the team were renovating the space.

All in all it's a charming and oddly romantic setting best visited by night when candlelight guides you in. Candlelight also offers a barely-there glow once inside past a heavy velvet curtain, allowing intimate dates to unfold in booths. The charcuterie hangs above the bar where pickles and cornichons sit in jars, while wine pours enthusiastically around the room. WC shines a light on different wine producers each month, and baked Camembert, pâté and tartiflette are there to complement the continental offerings by the glass. Make an evening of it – it's well worth spending more than a penny at WC.

Address Clapham Common South Side, SW4 7AA, +44 (0)20 7622 5502,
www.wcclapham.co.uk, info@wcclapham.co.uk | Getting there Clapham Common
(Northern Line) | Hours Mon–Thu 5–11.30pm, Fri 5pm–12.30am, Sat 3pm–12.30am,
Sun 3–10.30pm | Tip The reverse is Counter Culture restaurant over the road, which
doesn't even have its own toilet (you have to use the one in sister restaurant The Dairy).
But boy does it know good food – modern British tapas and only room for 15 guests.

110_ Wenlock Arms

A real neighbourhood pub now preserved

Beery blokes dive into some post-match analysis and a round of darts while a group of pensioners nab seats by the open fire to nurse a bottle of plonk. You get all walks of local life at the Wenlock Arms – from regulars who've been frequenting this Hoxton pub in the canal's Wenlock Basin for upwards of 70 years (David Beckham's granddad once included) to fresh faces keen to check out what a true London pub is really all about. So it's mad to think it all nearly ended for the treasured Wenlock back in 2010.

It's a tale that's dotted throughout this book; when the pub was put up for sale, developers took a fancy to its potential as luxury condos. What they got instead was a fight led by locals Tessa Norton and Sian Murphy. Their 'Save the Wenlock' passion prevailed when in December 2011 the council backed the cause, extending the Regent's Canal Conservation Area, protecting the pub's architectural and historic qualities in the deal.

And that they've certainly done. When the pub reopened under new landlords as a free house in 2013 the neighbourhood was delighted to find it restored to its former glory as a '19th-century ale house'. They even unearthed a 150-year-old mosaic spelling out the pub's name, now placed at the foot of the door. Beer is on the agenda more than ever, with 10 cask ales, 20 keg lines and 7 ciders on the bar (although Carlsberg is kept for the purists). But it's far from a chichi craft house – with its no-frills approach, authentic décor and simple cheese toasties, you can almost imagine the pub in its glory days, tied to the Wenlock brewery and run by locals (a Mitchell family even on the lease at one point, like something out of *EastEnders*).

During that campaign, Norton told the local press her reason for fighting to save the Wenlock Arms: 'I love this pub with all my stupid heart'. From one visit it's easy to see the attraction.

Address 26 Wenlock Road, N1 7TA, +44 (0)20 7608 3406, www.wenlockarms.com, beer@wenlockarms.com | **Getting there** Old Street (Northern Line, National Rail) | **Hours** Mon–Thu 3–11pm, Fri & Sat noon–1am, Sun noon–11pm | **Tip** The Victoria Miro (16 Wharf Road) is a contemporary art gallery in the area with its own canalside garden used as part of its exhibitions.

111 Ye Olde Cheshire Cheese

You won't brie-lieve its lesser-known history

Fire has marked this Fleet Street pub through its many years. Flames tore through the building in 1666 during the Great Fire of London, scorching over 100 years of pub history. A year later the pub reopened, and from a visit now it's clear that not a great deal has changed since – white-washed stone walls, low oak beams, dark wood panels and tall-backed benches hark back to the simpler London that Samuel Pepys had written so prolifically about.

Then it happened again in 1962: a fire – luckily not quite so 'great' – broke out on the upper storey. This made its impact felt in other ways, its devastation unveiling a few clues to the pub's then-unknown history. While the Cheshire Cheese was noted for the sacred ground it stood on – taking over the site of a Carmelite monastery from the 1300s – its famous inhabitants across the years may not have known about a more unholy past. In the wreckage of the fire, pornographic tiles were uncovered and historians have since commented that these sordid scenes may have been a sort of mood enhancer in an 18th-century gentlemen's club or maybe even a brothel upstairs. Sadly, the tiles have been squirreled away by the Museum of London rather than put on display in the pub.

What is on show is a chair dedicated to Dickens (let's face it, which historic London pubs didn't he drink in?), and a parrot in a cage – although not Polly the Parrot, the pub's rude squawker famous enough to have had an obituary in the international press in 1926. For these two reasons alone, the Cheese attracts many tourists come the weekend. But visit early in the week to see why Dickens and his literary peers – from Samuel Johnson and Mark Twain to Arthur Conan Doyle and P. G. Wodehouse – were lured in. There's a chop-house, a spit-and-sawdust bar and a maze of rooms connected by little darkened passageways (mind your head!) ideal for secluded drinking. And of course, a number of warming fireplaces.

Address 145 Fleet Street, EC4A 2BU, +44 (0)20 7353 6170, www.samuelsmithsbrewery.co.uk | Getting there City Thameslink (National Rail) | Hours Mon–Fri 11.30am–11pm, Sat noon–11pm | Tip Continue the Ye Olde theme: fellow City pub Ye Olde Mitre (1 Ely Place) similarly creaks with age.

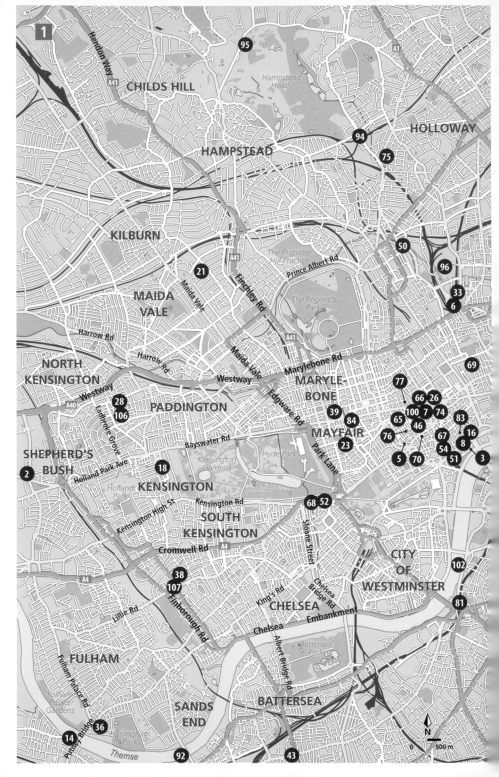

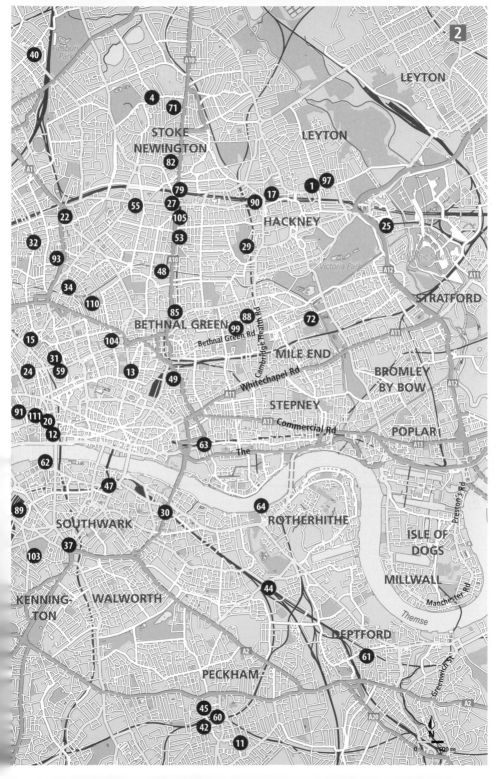

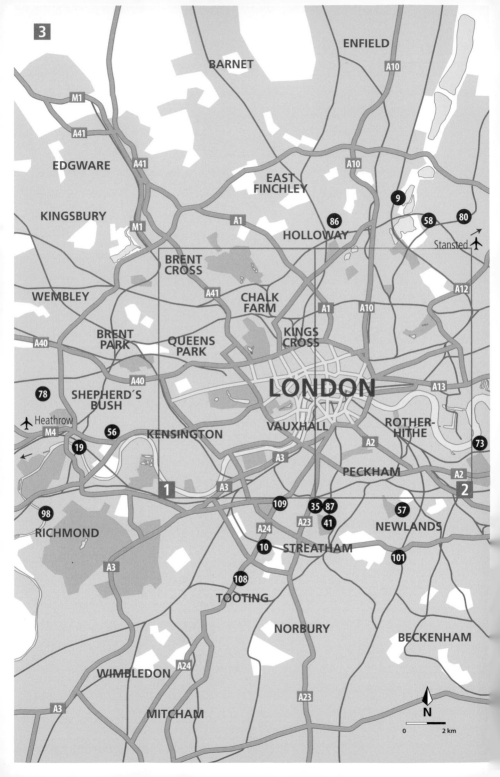

Lucia Jay von Seldeneck,
Carolin Huder, Verena Eidel
**111 PLACES IN BERLIN
THAT YOU SHOULDN'T MISS**
ISBN 978-3-95451-208-9

Rüdiger Liedtke
**111 PLACES IN MUNICH
THAT YOU SHOULDN'T MISS**
ISBN 978-3-95451-222-5

Rike Wolf
**111 PLACES IN HAMBURG
THAT YOU SHOULDN'T MISS**
ISBN 978-3-95451-234-8

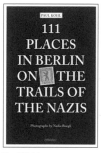

Paul Kohl
**111 PLACES IN BERLIN
ON THE TRAIL OF THE NAZIS**
ISBN 978-3-95451-323-9

Sharon Fernandes
**111 PLACES IN NEW DELHI
THAT YOU MUST NOT MISS**
ISBN 978-3-95451-648-3

Sally Asher, Michael Murphy
**111 PLACES IN NEW ORLEANS
THAT YOU MUST NOT MISS**
ISBN 978-3-95451-645-2

Gerd Wolfgang Sievers
**111 PLACES IN VENICE
THAT YOU MUST NOT MISS**
ISBN 978-3-95451-460-1

Petra Sophia Zimmermann
**111 PLACES IN VERONA
AND LAKE GARDA THAT
YOU MUST NOT MISS**
ISBN 978-3-95451-611-7

Gillian Tait
**111 PLACES IN EDINBURGH
THAT YOU SHOULDN'T MISS**
ISBN 978-3-95451-883-8

Laurel Moglen, Julia Posey
**111 PLACES IN LOS ANGELES
THAT YOU SHOULDN'T MISS**
ISBN 978-3-95451-884-5

John Sykes
**111 PLACES IN LONDON
THAT YOU SHOULDN'T MISS**
ISBN 978-3-95451-346-8

Julian Treuherz, Peter de Figueiredo
**111 PLACES IN LIVERPOOL
THAT YOU SHOULDN'T MISS**
ISBN 978-3-95451-769-5

Annett Klingner
111 PLACES IN ROME
THAT YOU MUST NOT MISS
ISBN 978-3-95451-469-4

Kirstin von Glasow
111 COFFEESHOPS IN
LONDON THAT YOU MUST
NOT MISS
ISBN 978-3-95451-614-8

Giulia Castelli Gattinara, Mario Verin
111 PLACES IN MILAN
THAT YOU MUST NOT MISS
ISBN 978-3-95451-331-4

Kirstin von Glasow
111 GARDENS IN LONDON
THAT YOU SHOULDN'T MISS
ISBN 978 3 7408 0143-4

Jo-Anne Elikann
111 PLACES IN NEW YORK
THAT YOU MUST NOT MISS
ISBN 978-3-95451-052-8

Kathrin Bielfeldt, Raymond Wong,
Jürgen Bürger
111 PLACES IN HONG KONG
THAT YOU SHOULDN'T MISS
ISBN 978-3-95451-936-1

Nicola Perry, Daniel Reiter
33 Walks in London
Photographs by Daniel Reiter
ISBN 978-3-95451-886-9

Ralf Nestmeyer
**111 PLACES IN PROVENCE
THAT YOU MUST NOT MISS**
ISBN 978-3-95451-422-9

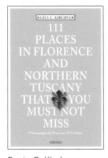

Beate C. Kirchner
**111 PLACES IN FLORENCE
AND NORTHERN TUSCANY
THAT YOU MUST NOT MISS**
ISBN 978-3-95451-613-1

Floriana Petersen, Steve Werney
**111 PLACES IN SAN FRANCISCO
THAT YOU MUST NOT MISS**
ISBN 978-3-95451-609-4

Ralf Nestmeyer
**111 PLACES ON THE
FRENCH RIVIERA
THAT YOU MUST NOT MISS**
ISBN 978-3-95451-612-4

Kirstin von Glasow
**111 SHOPS IN LONDON
THAT YOU SHOULDN'T MISS**
ISBN 978-3-95451-341-3

Acknowledgments

Thank you to Jamie for his ceaseless enthusiasm and energy; to Alison, whose comments in the margins kept me smiling; to Alistair for finding me such a fun job; and to Laura and the whole team at Emons. Thanks to my family for all their support – particularly Mum and Dad, who got me through that second deadline. And to Zoë, who has been a mentor, as well as a sister. And thanks to all my friends and pub-crawl recruits – without you, this book wouldn't have been possible or half as fun to write. In particular, thank you to Sophie and to Isobel for putting in the hard hours at the bar, to Abi, Kath, Laura, Liz and Hayley for pub-hopping with me, to Hannah and Matty for putting up with my late nights (writing and drinking) and to Belinda, Hannah, Lizzy and Robyn for sending support from afar. Thanks to Mark and Steve for letting me write about pubs and bars in the first place (my liver has something different to say to you). And thanks to London's brilliant landlords and landladies and to all the talented bar people who make London the best place to drink in the world. Cheers!

Laura Richards was born near Liverpool and grew up near Peterborough. She studied Spanish at the University of Bristol and in Zaragoza, Spain before moving to London to train as a journalist. She started out writing about pregnancy and parenting before a drastic change of pace, documenting the bar, club and restaurant scene in London. In her current role as Associate Editor and Drinks Editor at Time Out London, she visits the latest launches to uncover scene-defining bars and pubs. Her search for the perfect piña colada continues.

Jamie Newson is a freelance photographer residing in Farnham, Surrey. Having been used to the hustle of Essex where he grew up, he continues to take trips into the city where he works mostly photographing new food and newer people. He hopes to be photographing his way round London for as long as possible.